FOLK
CUSTOMS OF
CHINA

FOLK CUSTOMS OF CHINA

Text by Qiu Huanxing

Photographed by Lu Zhongmin and others

Foreign Languages Press Beijing

Text by Qiu Huanxing
Photographed by Lu Zhongmin and others
Edited by Liao Pin
Designed by Wang Zhi

First Edition 1992

ISBN 0-8351-2797-4
ISBN 7-119-01471-4

Copyright 1992 by Foreign Languages Press, Beijing, China

Published by Foreign Languages Press
24 Baiwanzhuang Road, Beijing 100037, China

Printed by Toppan Printing Co. (Singapore) Ltd.

Distributed by China International Book Trading Corporation
35 Chegongzhuang Xilu, Beijing 100044, China
P.O. Box 399, Beijing, China

Contents

A Sketch Map of Regions

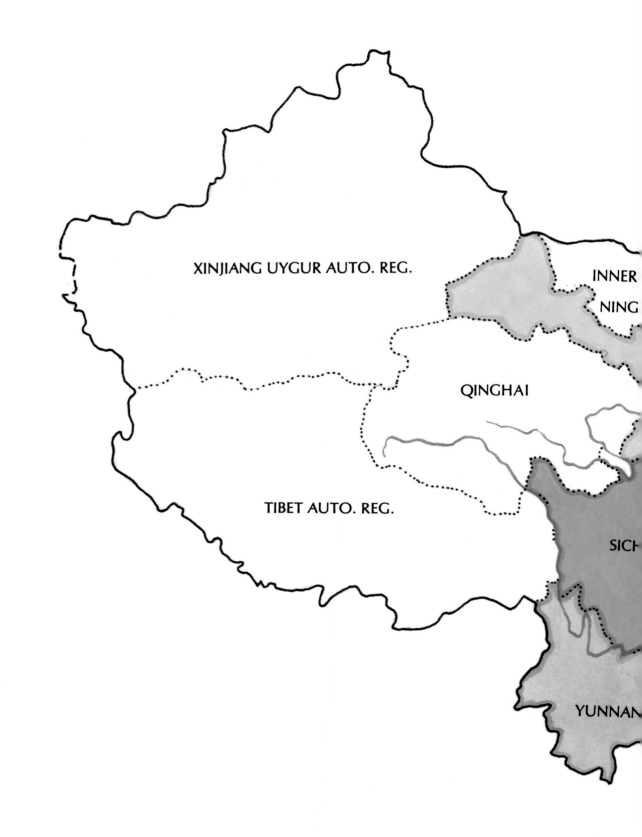

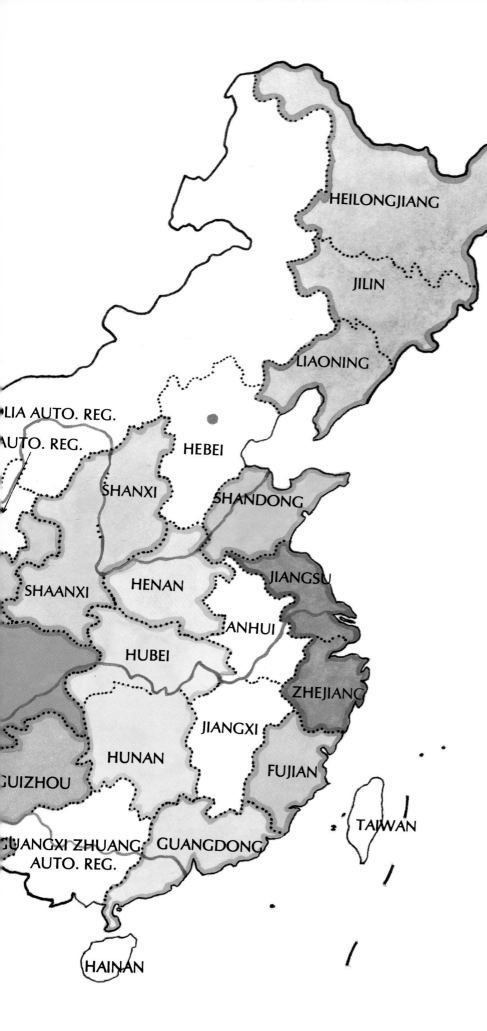

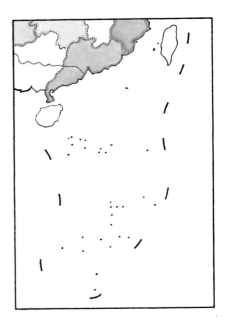

Preface

Every nation has its special characteristics resulting from a particular environment and cultural and historical development. Folk customs play an important role in the culture of an ethnic group. When we have contact with another culture, popular folk customs arouse our impressions most easily. The larger the difference between two nations, the stronger one's impressions will be.

Folk customs are not particular to only certain cultures, but exist universally in the social organization of all ethnic groups. They are manifested mainly in the forms of etiquette, customs, and the way the basic necessities of life are produced and distributed—food, clothing, shelter and transportation which affect the daily lives of any group. For example, the economic activities of individual and family organizations have become independent components of society; however, they were an integral part of the customs in primitive society. Though independent today, customary constellations still exist in organizations. Strictly speaking, there is no organization without any social and cultural customs. Folk customs exist widely and universally in society and they perform their own social functions.

This is the very reason why anthropology has been gaining more attention from international academics and researchers as a social science.

China has a vast territory with a long history. All kinds of social forms of organization developed and merged with other cultures. As a result, China has rich multi-cultural society of which we can get a hint of from this album. For example, the architectural style of houses varies greatly in the north and in the south. No doubt China's varied folk customs and cultures have enriched Chinese history and culture and serve as a warehouse of information in terms of the history of human culture.

Therefore, I feel that the compilation of this album *Folk Customs of China* is significant to the understanding of China's diverse cultures.

This album, though not a monumental work, is richly informative. It shows the material organization of different cultures, and reflects their spiritual and cultural activities too. It is a panorama of the folk customs of various cultures and regions in China from the *errenzhuan* (a song-and-dance duet) in the northeast to the terraced fields and round houses in the south; from the arch bridges, *wupeng* (black awning) boats and grass roofs in the east and southeast to the bamboo markets, papercuts and flower cakes in the west and northwest,—all kinds of folk customs all over China are described in a lively narrative tone. The cultures are varied and colourful, and the vigorous spirit and creative power of the people is unlimited.

The beautiful photographs and picturesque accounts will probably arouse the interest of folklorists, ethnologists or sociologists to explore further into their fields of study and will probably also arouse the curiosity of the layman. If so, this will turn out to be an accidental, but gratifying reward to those who compiled this album.

Zhong Jingwen*
September 24, 1990
Beijing Teachers University

---

*Born in 1903, Zhong Jingwen is a well-known folklorist and expert in folk customs studies. He had been dedicated to the research and teaching of folklore and folk literature for many years. His works include *On Folk Literature, Folk Literature Anthology of Zhong Jingwen, New Journey,* and *On Folk Culture.* He is a professor in the Department of Chinese in the Beijing Teachers University and concurrently chairman of the China Folk Writers' and Artists' Association, director-general of the Chinese Folk Customs Society and a member of the National Committee of the Chinese Federation of Literary and Art Circles.

13

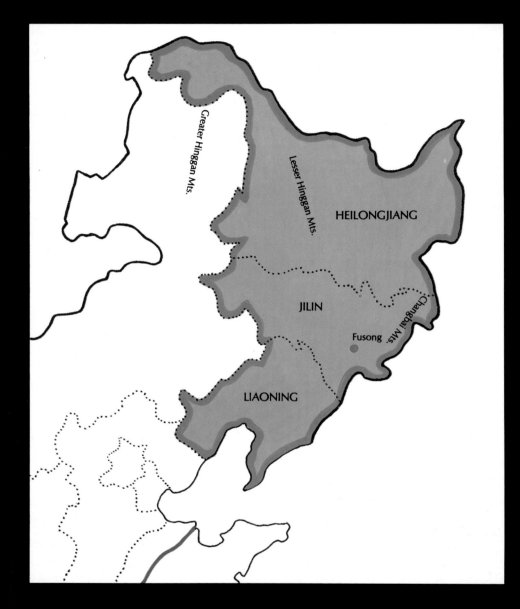

Greater Hinggan Mts.

Lesser Hinggan Mts.

HEILONGJIANG

JILIN

Changbai Mts.

Fusong

LIAONING

I. Local Customs in China's Northeast

THE most important and popular of the traditional holidays in China is the Spring Festival, or the Chinese New Year. It falls on the first day of each lunar year. The history of celebrating the Spring Festival goes back more than 3,000 years. Today, people, especially in rural areas, still celebrate the Chinese New Year rather than the New Year's Day of the Gregorian calendar which was adopted in China in 1912. The Chinese refer to January 1 as New Year's Day and the first day of the first month by the lunar calendar as the Spring Festival. Officially, people only get three or four days off for the holiday, but people in the countryside celebrate it for a whole month.

The Chinese New Year is celebrated in much the same way all over the country. The one I spent in a small mountain village of Jilin Province in the Northeast is quite typical.

As the three provinces of Heilongjiang, Jilin and Liaoning are located in Northeast China, they are often known as the Northeast, or *Guandong*, (East of the Pass), for they are situated to the east of the Shanhai Pass, located at the east end of the Great Wall.

Spring Festival in a Village

I went to a village called Fulu where 63 families live. By the time I got there, it was already the 27th of the 12th lunar month. On my way I saw that the gates of almost every house were decorated with green pine needles and red Chinese lanterns. People rode in horse carriages back from a country fair with packages of goods for the holiday. Though students were on vacation, the playground of the school reverberated with the deafening sound of gongs and drums; a group of young people were rehearsing *yangge*, a local folk dance, and some others were walking on stilts.

After I arrived at Fulu Village, I stayed with a family named Liu. On that day they were making buns to eat, a must for the Spring Festival in the north. The buns were made of glutinous millet flour and stuffed with sweetened bean paste. After they were steamed, they were taken to be stored outside of the house and would be reheated or deep-fried later. Before Spring Festival, every family made enough buns to last for a month. Whenever someone was going to make the buns, all he needed to do was to tell his neighbours and they were always ready to help. Sitting on the heated *kang* (brick bed), chatting and laughing, they finished making the buns in no time. After the first batch of buns came out of the steamer, the hostess asked everyone to taste the soft and delicious buns.

It is customary that people start to prepare for the Spring Festival from as early as the twelfth month of the lunar year. On the eighth day of the month, every family eats a special gruel known as "eight-treasure porridge" which is made of rice, millet, glutinous rice, sorghum, red beans, peanuts, dates, walnuts and brown sugar. Originally a gruel for Buddhists to commemorate Sakyamuni's attainment of nirvana, it is eaten in the hope that it will bring a bumper harvest in the coming year. On this day, some people pour the gruel on the roots of the fruit trees in their yards because it is believed that if the trees "eat" some gruel, they will bear more fruit.

The 23rd of the twelfth month is the day for the Kitchen God. In the old days, every household would put up a poster of the Kitchen God above the kitchen range with a couplet on each side that read: "Saying good words in Heaven / Making peace stay on earth." Legend goes that the Kitchen God was the brother of the celestial Jade Emperor. Every year on the 23rd of the twelfth month when the Kitchen God got together with the Jade Emperor, he would report the behaviour of each household, and the Jade Emperor would punish or reward them accordingly. So on this day for the Kitchen God a table on which to burn incense was set up at every house on which malt sugar and dishes were offered as sacrificial objects and a flying horse made from cornstalks was on the table too, so the Kitchen God could ride to Heaven. It was believed that if the Kitchen God ate the sweet malt sugar, he would report more good things in Heaven. The last part of the ritual was when the host prayed, "Kitchen God, please put in a few good words for us when you see the Jade Emperor in Heaven." After he finished the prayer, he would send the Kitchen God to Heaven by burning the poster that had been blackened by smoke throughout the year.

The following day, every family became even busier. Husbands started to buy Spring Festival goods and liquor and kill chickens and ducks, while the wives began to clean the house, sew new clothes, make New Year cakes and other delicacies.

The eve of the Spring Festival is the busiest day of the year and I could feel the festive atmosphere strongly. In the morning, every family started to put up what is called "spring couplets," a custom practised everywhere in China. The spring couplet consists of two pieces of red paper on which lucky sayings are written. The couplet is generally pasted on doors or on each side of the frame and the content varies depending on whose room the couplet is to be pasted. For instance, on the bedroom door of Liu's mother, the couplet read, "Heaven and people get one year older / May the spring fill the world and happiness fill the house." On the door of Liu's bedroom, the couplet said, "Heaven, land and people are benevolent / The auspicious spring snow promises a good harvest." On the door of the barn, the couplet read, "Sowing one seed in spring / Harvesting ten thousand piculs of grain in autumn." The couplets were even posted on the sides of carts and at the horse shed: "Travel a thousand miles / May the people and horse be blessed with peace," and "Oxen are as vigorous as tigers in the south mountain / Horses are as powerful as the dragon in the north sea." At this time of the year, the biggest wish of the peasants is to have a bumper harvest and thriving livestock.

As the Chinese saying goes, "On festive occasions more than ever people think of their family and friends living far away." Spring Festival is a time that always reminds people of their ancestors who, dead and buried, must feel very lonely. Therefore, people bring incense and firecrackers to their graves to hold memorial ceremonies. At home, they set up an incense burner table on which they place various sacrificial objects. Above the table hangs a piece of paper with all their ancestors' names on it.

After the ceremony, the whole family sits on the heated *kang* and starts the Spring Festival Eve's dinner by making toasts while the deafening noise of firecrackers goes on outside. The dinner is an occasion for which family members living far away are supposed to come back home.

The most sumptuous dinner of the year, it consists of certain dishes that signify good wishes of the family. In Chinese, fish has the same pronunciation as the word for abundance, therefore fish is always served in the hope that the family will have more than enough money to spend. A bowl of meatballs in brown sauce is a symbol for family

1

16

1   With a long and cold winter, the Northeast is situated in northernmost China. In winter, when the ground is covered by ice and snow and the rivers are frozen, horse–driven sleighs are the main means of transportation.

unity.

After dinner, it is time to give children money as a Spring Festival gift, a moment that children look forward to. Elder members of the family hand out money wrapped in red paper. The children can buy candies, firecrackers, picture books and anything they like with the money.

On the Spring Festival Eve, people generally stay up all night to welcome the New Year. In the Northeast in the old days the eldest member of the family always sat on the upper end of the heated *kang*, telling stories, riddles and jokes; men and women would get together to play cards or mahjong; boys would take their paper lanterns and go to other people's yards to light firecrackers. But now people just sit in front of the TV watching the Spring Festival specials.

It is also customary for many Chinese minority nationalities to stay up all night on Spring Festival Eve, though it is practised in different ways. In the Northeast, the Daurs sing and dance the whole night, while young Oroqen men courteously bow and propose toasts to their parents and grandparents. The Tujias and Bouyeis in the south sit around a fire in the open for the whole night. The Tujias would sit on weeds as it is believed that weeds can be killed by sitting on them. Bouyei girls always get up early in the morning to try to be the first one to carry back a bucket of water which is said to symbolize wisdom.

The New Year comes as the clock strikes twelve. Then every family starts a fire in the yard and lights firecrackers to illuminate the cold, dark sky.

People come out again in the early morning to light firecrackers to see out the old year and welcome the new year. This is a custom which has been observed for over 2,000 years. Legend has it that, long ago, there was a beast called *nian* (year) that was bigger than a camel and could run very fast. Because the *nian* ate people wherever they went, the Heavenly God locked it in remote mountains and allowed it to come out only on New Year's Eve. On this night, people would come out with knives and clubs to fight the *nian*.

2   Before the Spring Festival, every household cleans the house. After that, people removed the antithetical couplets, window papercuts and New Year pictures put up in the previous year. At this time, picture stands at the market flourish everywhere.

2

Gradually it was discovered that *nians* were afraid of red–coloured things, flames and noise. From then on, people always put up red couplets, made fires or lit firecrackers to scare away the *nian* who would then starve to death in mountain caves.

When the firecrackers are lit, it is time to make *jiaozi*, or New Year *jiaozi*, a special food for the Spring Festival in North China. The filling is generally made of ground meat mixed with vegetables and is wrapped in a thin and round piece of dough. *Jiaozi* are shaped like crescent moons. The hostess puts a clean coin in one of the *jiaozi*. It is believed that the person who happens to eat this special *jiaozi* will have good luck. In some places, people put red dates or peanuts or candies inside instead. Peanuts, also called the longevity nut, symbolizes a long life. Red dates and candies mean prosperity and happiness for the coming year.

In South China, people have *wonton* dumplings for the festival. In Mandarin Chinese, *wonton* is pronounced as *huntun* which sounds like two other Chinese characters meaning "storing plenty of grain." In some places, noodles, the symbol of longevity, are served; in other places, *tangyuan*, a round dumpling made of glutinous rice flour, is served, as it stands for family reunion. For Buddhists, no meat is allowed on this day because they think that this is the day when Buddha opens his eyes and he would not be happy to see meat being served.

After eating *jiaozi*, it is time to pay New Year calls to the elders who all sit on the *kang* accepting good wishes from their family.

When day breaks, villagers go out to pay New Year calls to the old people in the

3   When making *doubao* (dumplings with mashed bean filling), neighbours help each other.

20

4   Offerings to ancestors are all arranged by the elders who have high prestige in the community.

5   The genealogy is hung on the wall at the annual Spring Festival for all the family members to offer sacrifices and pay their respects to their ancestors.

5

village. When people meet on the way, they bow and wish each other a happy New Year. They believe that even if two enemies meet at this moment, they should bury the hatchet and become friends by wishing one another a happy New Year.

The history of paying New Year calls goes back to the time when people had to chase away the beast *nian*. On the morning of New Year's Day when they met and saw that they had survived the *nian*, they were so happy they started to congratulate each other.

During the Song Dynasty (960–1279), the gentry and intelligentsia thought it a waste of time to pay New Year calls door to door and that it was almost impossible to convey greetings to relatives and friends living far away. So someone came up with the idea of sending New Year cards. The notes were sent on a piece of paper with a plum blossom drawn on it, and the note was sent by servants or postmen. So today's practice of sending New Year cards probably originated from that custom.

Stilt teams also pay New Year calls to villages. Each team consists of 20 to 30 people. A band walks in the front and is followed by a group of young men and women in classical costumes with colourful fans and silk ribbons in their hands and one–metre high stilts bound on their feet. The lion and dragon dancers at the rear of the procession are mostly strong young men in their twenties or thirties.

The singers on the stilt team go to each house and pay New Year calls by giving impromptu performances. People dance to the beat of the drums and gongs in the yard. A joker threads his way through the dancers while making fun of himself to amuse the audience. The performances have not only built closer relations between villages but are also entertaining people during the festival season.

6   On the eve of the Spring Festival, couplets are pasted on the gateposts of every family.

7   During the Spring Festival, every household sets up wooden poles to hang big, red lanterns on. Nighttime is beautiful as the red lanterns set off the white snow.

8   A home–made woodblock print of the Kitchen God includes his wife and attendants.

9   *A Joyful View on the Eve of the Spring Festival*, a painting from the Qing Dynasty, depicts a scene of rich people in North China celebrating the Spring Festival Eve 100 years ago.

6

7

10   On the eve of the Spring Festival, every household sets off fireworks. In the past, people set off fireworks for the purpose of dispelling evil, but now it has become a form of entertainment.

11   The picture *Paying New Year Calls* describes the tradition of visiting friends and relatives at Spring Festival time in the Song Dynasty which began more than 800 years ago.

12   On the morning of the Lunar New Year's Day, *yangge* troupes go into the street dressed in colourful costumes.

10

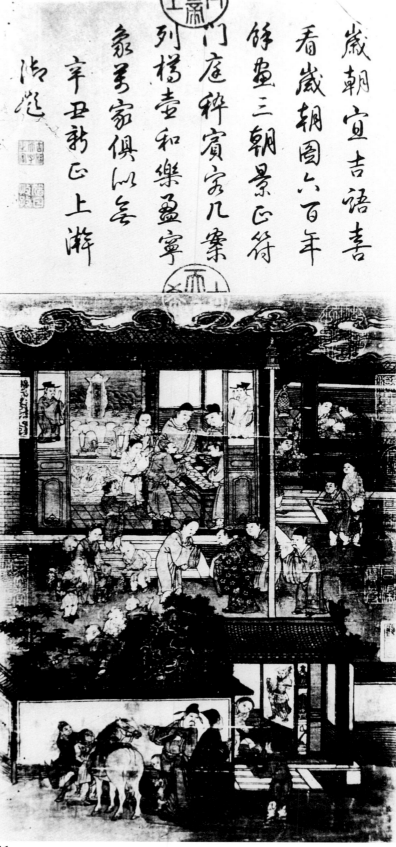

11

13

13 The stilt team visits villages to pay New Year calls to the villagers.

14 Performers walk on stilts, jumping, spinning, and running quickly even on snow-covered roads.

14

15

15 *Errenzhuan* (a popular song and dance duet) is performed in people's homes. *Errenzhuan* is performed by a man and a woman who also dance while singing. Because of the lively performance and the songs about the local life, *Errenzhuan* is loved by the farmers.

The "Five Rarities" in the Northeast Villages

Straw-walled houses are surrounded by wooden fences,
Paper is pasted outside the lattice windows,
Chimney stems from the gable,
New-born babies are hung from a cradle on the beam,
Girls go about with long pipes in their mouths.

This is a folk rhyme popular in China's north. The "five rarities" are so called because these practices look unique in the eyes of those who come to the Northeast for the first time.

South of the Great Wall, houses, are built with earthen bricks or bricks fried in a kiln. But in the Northeast, rice straw is mixed with mud to make bricks. To build the wall, wooden poles standing 60 centimetres from each other, are buried in the foundation of the house. Plaits as thick as bowls and made of rice straw mixed with mud are wound around the poles. Then mud is spread on the inside and outside of the poles and is braided up to the ceiling. After the wall is built, roof beams and rafters are set. A screen made of twigs is laid on the roof before mud is spread on it. To complete the new house, a layer of hay about 20 centimetres thick is put on the mud. As rice straw preserves heat very well, it is warm inside the house in winter times. However, it takes too much time to build the house and the outside of it doesn't look very nice. Besides, the inside of the walls makes an ideal place for mice to build their nests. Because of the above-mentioned disadvantages, the straw wall has been replaced by earthen bricks or bricks from kilns, except that the old way of putting hay on the roof to preserve heat is still kept. A wooden fence is also set up around every house.

Although glass is now widely used for windows in North China, sometimes a kind of thin but pliable and tenacious white paper is pasted inside of the lattice window. In the Northeast, it was pasted outside of the window and has now been replaced by double-glass window. When I asked people why the paper was pasted outside instead of inside the lattice window, they told me that it was to prevent strong winds from breaking the paper. Besides, the paper pasted outside could withstand much greater pressure and could keep the snow and dust from landing on the lattice and blocking the sunlight.

It is very common for the northern peasants to sleep on a heated platform called a *kang*. Generally, there is only one *kang* in the room. But in the Northeast, the *kang* is built all around the room. The kitchen stove is connected with the tunnel under the *kang*, so that during cooking the heat can go through it to warm up the *kang* before the smoke goes out from the chimney at the gable.

When the Northeasterners build their homes, they always put a beam above the *kang* so that a cradle could be hung on it. The mother always puts the baby in the cradle while doing housework around the house. Besides, they believe that it is not good for the baby to sleep on the *kang* because too much heat might cause "internal fire" in the baby and make him sick.

The habit of girls smoking long-stemmed pipes has to do with the cold weather. In the past during the wintertime and the slack season, women would sit on the *kang* all day long, either sewing, cracking sunflower seeds, or smoking the very strong Northeast tobacco. However, young women with pipes can rarely be seen now, although once in a while old women in two or three smoking long-stemmed pipes can still be found.

17

18

19

20

16 A farmer's courtyard in the Northeast.

17 A three-side *kang* is not only a bed for sleeping at night, but it is also a general living space used by children for their homework and by the women for sewing and embroidery, and the family also eats on it and receives guests there as well.

18 In the hammock, a child may lie or sit, comfortable like being in a boat.

19 It is difficult to find a girl smoking a pipe now, but older women who smoke pipes can still be seen.

20 Young peasant girls.

Forest Scenes

The Greater and Lesser Hinggan Mountains in Heilongjiang and the Changbai Mountains in the east of Jilin Province are major forested areas in China. Many wild plants and animals live in the dense forests. Precious fur clothing, rare herbal medicines and special forest products are also found here.

I stayed for a few days at Changsong Village in Fusong County in the Changbai Mountains and what I saw was quite different from my experience in the Northeast countryside.

The houses of the 90-odd families at Changsong Village were either built in the mountain or by the river. Almost everything, fences, houses, storehouses and sheds, is made of wood. What surprised me most was that the chimney was a round and seamless tree trunk four to five metres high. The wood is known as *fengdao*, an overripe tree. The outerside of the tree is hard and does not catch fire easily, while the innerside is inflammable and is therefore hollowed out by burning the centre with a slow fire from the root.

Though a wooden house preserves warmth and resists earthquakes, it catches fire easily and uses up a large amount of timber. In recent years, brick houses have become more popular.

Winter is the best season to fell trees because at this time of year, trees are crisp and easy to chop, and the snow in the mountain makes it more convenient to pull the tree trunks with sleighs.

It was the first time for me to go into the forest. Treading the narrow path covered with snow, I became exhausted after a little while. When I saw a stump, I swept the snow off. But as I was about to sit on it, the mountain villagers warned me not to sit on it because it was believed to be the chair of the Mountain God, which is an imaginary god that the mountain villagers worship. There is no statue of him or temple for him. In the past when the woodcutters went to the mountain, they would first set up a makeshift "temple" with three rocks or plywood. But if they could not find these, they would simply chisel out a house-shaped pattern on one of the tree trunks.

The rock in the centre symbolizes the god of the tiger. Only by worshipping this god, could people be safe from tigers. The rocks on either side are said to represent the "God of the Five Ways" and the "God of Earth" that can protect people from disaster. They use pine torches as candles and mountain grass as incense to worship these gods.

The worship of the Mountain God originated from the fear of the forest in the old days when there was no protective measures for the woodcutters. If they were careless, they would either be crushed to death or wounded by a falling tree, or their head would be broken by the dead branches which the locals call "hanging ghosts"; or they would be wounded by an axe or saw, or stumble and fall, or even be attacked by tigers and bears. Unable to master nature, these woodcutters had to turn to gods for solace and relief from danger.

Every year during Spring Festival time, it was customary to cut down the first tree of the year, in order to predict the fortune of the year. On New Year's Day, after worshipping the Mountain God, they would gather at the tree previously chosen as the first tree, generally a straight, well-rounded and hard Korean pine. The ceremony began with a prayer and then people took turns to cut the tree with an axe. With a tremendous boom, the tree fell obediently downhill. If the tree didn't fall on other tree branches or hurt anyone, people felt more at ease; the new year would be a peaceful one.

Today, woodcutters all wear safety helmets and they are not afraid of the falling

21   In the Changbai Mountains, villagers build houses with wood.

22   A little house in the forest.

23   A cellar where forest rangers live, half underground and half above ground.

21

22

23

"hanging ghosts" any more. Machines are used for felling, collecting and transporting timber. As a result, accidents have greatly decreased. Though they don't worship the Mountain God as much as they used to, they still do not sit on stumps or fell the trees that bear the mark of "Mountain God Temple."

Many animals and birds also inhabit the dense forests of the Changbai Mountains such as Northeast tigers, bears, boars, lynxes, sika deer, musk deer, red deer, sables, racoons, roe deer and pheasants. Except tigers, musk deer, deer, lynxes and sables which are under state protection, other animals and birds are all hunted.

In early winter when snow covers up grass and fallen leaves, hunters bring along their food and cooking utensils and go into the mountains to hunt. As soon as they set up the camp in the mountain, they also built a "Mountain God Temple."

Hunters use hounds to hunt animals in early winter. When they hear the bark of the hound, they know that a bear has been found in its lair. Bears generally start to look for a lair as soon as winter starts. The small deft bears all go into holes in dead trees, but the clumsy big ones have to dig a pit in the ground, which makes it easy for the hounds to scent them out.

When the hunter takes aim at the dead tree's hole, other hunters go up and knock the tree with their axes so that the shocked bear crawls out. When half of its body is out of the hole, the hunter kills it. While the bear is still warm, they immediately skin it and cut its chest open to take out the bear's gallbladder and chop off the bear's paws. Then they disembowel the bear to reward the hounds. The winter hunting season ends when the snow is over a foot deep, making it hard for hunters and hounds to run around.

Early spring is also good time for hunting when snow melts during the day but freezes into thin ice at night and in the early morning. The boar's heavy body, tiny feet and short legs make it impossible for it to run fast enough on the ice and as soon as they touch the thin ice, they get stuck in the snow.

The hound is agile and can run very fast. Hunters usually bind two "running rings" made of willow twigs to their feet, so that they can run on thin ice without falling. When they catch up with the boar, they either use the hounds to bit them or poke them with their dagger without firing any shots.

When the sun comes out and the ice melts, hunters go back to their camp. A few men from the hunting team carry the prey back to their village. If there is too much prey that cannot be taken back all at once, the hunters cover it with snow. Otherwise, they would attract crows which would eat them.

As the tiger is said to be the Mountain God, it is forbidden to shoot them. Before they start out, hunters have to say prayers for the tiger. The heart and liver of the first prey caught in the year are cooked and offered to the tiger, the Mountain God, before the hunters are allowed to touch it. Although this practice is superstitious, in a way it has protected the Northeast tiger, an endangered species.

When the hunters leave the mountain, they also leave firewood and salt in the camp for anyone who might get lost in the mountain.

Those who are familiar with the habits of the animals also use snares to trap the animal and they hang wood which sometimes hits the animal. The most interesting of all is catching the otter by freezing it. Hunters usually place an iron board near the ice hole where otters frequently go. At midnight when they come out from the river, where they have just eaten some fish or frogs, and jump onto the board to lick off the water, the water from their body soon freezes and makes them stick to the board, making it very easy for the hunters to catch them.

24

24 Inside a cellar. The skylight lets the sunlight in. A log walls are constructed to prevent wetness.

25 In winter, hunters riding a sleigh go hunting in the forests with hounds.

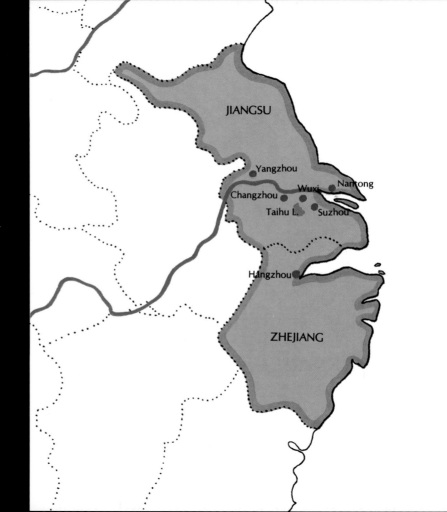

II. A Region of Rivers and Lakes

ONE spring, I went to a region of rivers and lakes in Jiangsu and Zhejiang provinces to collect folk stories. The region is situated on the south banks of the largest river in China, the Yangtze River, so it is often called "water country south of the Yangtze," including southern Jiangsu Province with Taihu Lake at its centre and eastern Zhejiang Province. It is a typical lake region, with scattered lakes and a network of waterways.

Bridges and Boats

There are many bridges in the region. Some are high bridges with arches like a crescent moon, some are slabstone bridges, some rainbow–shaped reinforced concrete bridges, and some are long and thin arch bridges. There are over 5,000 large and small stone bridges in the city of Shaoxing in Zhejiang Province, therefore, Shaoxing is renowned as a museum of ancient stone bridges.

The bridge for pedestrians is called Taiping (peace) bridge or Ankang (safe and healthy) bridge, to wish pedestrians safety in travelling. The bridge near grocery stores is named Jinli (making profit) bridge or Jinding (golden tripod) bridge, to wish for a brisk business. The bridge in the vicinity of some temples is known as Jishan (accumulating kindness) bridge or Xianghua (fragrant incense) bridge, meaning that those temples will have many worshippers. The Ke bridge, Xie bridge, Hong bridge, and others, are named for famous families.

Many ancient bridges are decorated with carved stone lions at the ends or columns of these bridges. It is an ancient Chinese custom to place the stone lions there which presumably can frighten away water monsters that cause disastrous floods.

At one time, superstitious people believed that God of Bridges existed. On New Year's Day or other festivals, some of the older women brought joss sticks, candles and paper money to bridges, as offerings to the God of Bridges for stable bridges, safe passengers and boats. When a pregnant woman was about to give birth, her family would carry several pounds of noodles to cross over three bridges. It was believed that the woman and the baby would be safe and healthy after she ate the noodles. When a rich and influential family held a funeral procession, a temporary ceremonial gateway would be constructed with pines and green bamboo, with paper flowers placed at the ends of the bridges which the procession would pass, as a symbol hoping the person would have happiness in the afterlife.

These old customs have all disappeared now. On festivals, however, local residents still decorate the main bridges with pines, cypresses, colourful flags and festive lanterns. After a night snowfall in winter, some people go to clean the snow from the bridges the next morning or spread husks of grain on the surface of the bridges in case someone slips and falls. In summer people like to sit on the bridges, enjoying the cool air, chatting, watching the lights of fishing boats on the river, in the gentle swaying breeze. The cares of the day are relieved by the tranquility of the scene.

Boats are the main means of transportation in the region and are as important as buses in the north, hence there is the Chinese saying: "boats in the south and buses in the north." Factories, government institutions and shops in cities and towns have their own boats besides those of shipping companies. The backdoors of many factories face the water, so boats can reach the doors directly.

Villagers depend on boats. They use boats as transportation to go to work and to go to town and visit friends in other places. Therefore, every household has a boat. It doesn't cost much to buy a small boat. It is even cheaper than buying a bicycle if you borrow a mold of a boat and pour cement into it to make a boat.

Though in the same village, when a bridegroom goes to his bride's home to escort her to the wedding, people will take several boats: a dowry boat transporting cupboards, clothes, and wooden basins, a boat with a pipe and drum band, a passenger boat for those who welcome the bride and offer congratulations. Although the bridal sedan chair is not popular now, the bride still sits on a bamboo chair and is carried to a boat by four young men. According to local custom, a wedding ceremony must be held at night. Many people like to get married at Spring Festival. At that time, fleets decorated with colourful lanterns can often be seen on the rivers at night, with the band playing music.

As well as bridges, there are various boats in the region, including wooden sailboats, cement boats, motor boats and fleets of freight barges sometimes over 1,000 metres long.

On the rivers around Shaoxing there is a kind of willowleaf-shaped boat, which is four metres long and one metre wide. Since its roofing is painted black, it is called *wupeng* (black awning) boat. The boat can generally hold two or three persons, six at most. The method of rowing the boat is unique. The boatman sits on the stern, paddling the boat with his feet. He carries the oar under his arm which he only uses to turn the boat. So, local residents also call the boat *jiaohuachuan* (boat paddled with feet). The cabin of this kind of boat is very short and narrow, so people can barely sit up straight in the cabin. However, the awning can be opened on a fine day, to enjoy the beautiful scenery along the banks of the river. When the boat with its small and light body sails on the surface of water, it is fun to slap the water with the hands. It is very interesting to travel on this sort of boat.

26

27

26   An early spring scene in the
"water country" south of the
Yangtze River.

27   Densely distributed bridges in
the "water country."

28

28 A bridge with one arch.

29 An arched bridge was built at one end of the flat slabstone bridge for boats to pass through.

30 Three- or five-arch bridges are commonly seen in the "water country."

31 The *lianjia* (connected home) bridge connects the dwellings separated by the river.

There are 60,000 or 70,000 people who actually live on boats for generations on Taihu Lake which is located in both Jiangsu and Zhejiang provinces. Their boats look like houses on land. The boats, usually about 24 metres long and four metres wide, have a dozen cabins, including a tool cabin for storing fishing tackle, a large cabin for fish and lobsters, a storage cabin for food, a kitchen cabin and bedroom cabins. These boats have many masts and sails and are quite similar to the warships of ancient times. It is said that the ancestors of the boat dwellers were members of the waterborne army led by General Yue Fei of the Southern Song Dynasty (1127-1279). When the army was preparing to defend the country from enemies, Yue Fei was framed by a treacherous minister, Qin Kuai, and was killed. When they heard the bad news, the officers and men got angry: "We don't want to die for the fatuous emperor and villainous ministers." Since they had no land and houses, they had to live on the warships and fish for a living. In this way, they created over 50 fishing villages along the banks of Taihu Lake. So that is why fishing boats on Taihu Lake look somewhat like the warships of ancient times.

It is a happy event for boat dwellers in the lake region to buy a new boat. A launching ceremony is always done for a new boat. At that time, on the door of the cabin a red

29

30

41

31

32 Built in the ninth century, the 53-arch Baodai (Jade Belt) Bridge is 370 metres long and looks like a jade belt.

32

Chinese character *xi* (happiness) will be placed and the cabin is filled with all kinds of food symbolizing prosperity and good fortune. The indispensable *jubaopen* (treasure bowl) is full of cakes made of glutinous rice in all shapes, such as carps, pomegranates, bamboo shoots and evergreen trees. The words for these items sound like the words for good fortune in Chinese. What is more, people will light red candles and set off firecrackers according to tradition.

Compared with driving a vehicle on land, it is much more dangerous to sail a boat on the water. Factors like a sudden storm, a damaged boat, and ineffective devices may cause an accident, capsizing the boat and killing people. In the times when there were no weather forecasts and modern communications, people could predict the weather only according to experience and communicated to each other by waving lanterns. In the struggle against nature to survive, some customs developed from superstitions. For example, boat dwellers or those who often took boats often refrained from saying words related to accidents such as *fu zhou* (a boat capsizing), *chen* (sinking), or *fan* (overturning), *qi huo* (catching fire), and *fu shi* (floating bodies). They even didn't say words which were similar in meaning or pronunciation to these phrases. Some boat dwellers carved the characters for the Jade Emperor, Queen Mother of the West Heaven, (Tathagata Buddha), and Goddess of Mercy on the lintel of doors, which were gods who give blessings.

33 There are many bridges on the river.

33

34

35

34   Pedestrians walk hastily on a bridge, while boats shutter under it.

35   In a town south of the Yangtze River, shops and buildings are all built beside the river. Boats are the main form of transportation.

36   *Wupeng* (black awning) boats on the river in the city of Shaoxing in Zhejiang Province.

37   The way to row the *Wupeng* boat is unique. A boatman sits on the stern, paddling the boat with his feet. He carries the oar under his arm to steer and turn the boat.

36

37

38 A stage is set up by the water in Shaoxing in Zhejiang Province. Villagers coming to see the performance row their *wupeng* boats to the front of the stage.

39 A stage built in an open square is often called *yetai* (field stage) in Zhejiang and Jiangsu provinces.

38

45

39

40

41

40 It is said that these fishing boats with several masts were developed from ancient warships.

41 The boat convoy is called "floating train" by the local people.

42 Whenever a new boat is launched, fishermen light red candles and put cakes and fruits as symbols of prosperity and good fortune in the cabin, along with a launching ceremony.

43

43 Fishermen hang four pieces of red and green silk on the side of the boat as a symbol for an abundant catch and a wish for more boats.

44 Kitchen cabin on a fishing boat.

45 The floating bridal chamber is prettily-decorated.

46 The densely distributed villages and towns in the "water country" form a sharp contrast to the sparsely distributed villages and towns in the Northeast.

44

45

46

Silkworm Raisers' Customs

Zhejiang and Jiangsu provinces are prominent silkworm producers in China. In early May each year, every household begins preparing to breed silkworms when barley becomes yellow and the mulberry fields turn green.

A dust-sized silkworm ovum will grow into an ant-shaped silkworm after brooding for a month, and then grow into a long white worm after four periods of quiescence and exuviation and then, the silkworm begins spinning pure white silk and finally turns into a pupa. There are many legends about the development of silkworms. One of them is a touching story which goes as follows.

Once upon a time, there was a father and his daughter who depended on each other very much. They had a white horse which the girl fed with mulberry leaves. Once, the father went out to do some trade and didn't come back on time. No one knew of his whereabouts. The daughter was very worried about him. One day, she prayed to marry a kind-hearted man who could help her find her father. When she had just finished asking for this, the white horse standing beside her nodded, circled around her three times and galloped away. Several days later, the white horse found the old man who had lost his way in the mountains and carried him home on his back. However, the white horse was always with the girl from then on and the father was puzzled by the matter. After he questioned her, the girl told the truth to her father. He got very angry, "It is natural that the horse looks for its owner, but how can an animal be a match for a person?" When the horse heard this, it began neighing and refused to eat anything. The father was very angry, and killed it with an arrow. He skinned the horse and dried the hide in the sunshine. After the daughter collected mulberry leaves, she returned home. Caressing the skin of the horse, she burst into tears. When her tears dropped on the horse, her body was wrapped up by the skin and flown to the sky. Later, seeing snow-white silkworms hanging on the mulberry trees, people said that these silkworms were the girl wrapped in the horse's skin. Since the head of the silkworm is similar to that of a horse's head, *Matouniang* (a girl with a horse's head) became another name for silkworm. When the daughter missed her father, she spun out the long silk. This is a legend about the origin of how silkworms spin silk and become silkworm cocoons.

In the past, whenever there was a bumper harvest of silkworm cocoons sericulturists would light an incense burner and offerings were arranged in the central room of a house to thank the Goddess of Silkworms. The statue of the goddess engraved on a wooden plate was a goddess in a horse-skin cloth. She had a vertical eye on her forehead which was deliberately drawn because no one could bear to see the arrow wound.

It is very interesting that Japan also has a legend about *Matouniang* with the spread of Chinese silkworms to Japan in the third century. However, in Japan the Goddess of Silkworms is a Japanese beauty in a kimono who rides a horse.

Sericulture in the region of Jiangsu and Zhejiang provinces is as important as farming. A good or poor harvest of silkworms is directly related to the livelihood of sericulturists. Silkworms are tender and delicate, hard to raise and easily get diseases. If the diseases spread, all the efforts of the sericulturists will be wasted. Therefore, when the season for breeding silkworms comes, every household in the villages is very busy. There are also many taboos and regulations in this period.

There are taboos surrounding the raising of silkworms. Women are prohibited from visiting friends, children from shouting, and men from going without a shirt during the time when silkworms are being hatched. On seeing peach branches which are thought to avoid evil and red paper with the characters *can yue zhi li* (A man should be polite in the month of silkworms) inserted on the eaves of a sericulturist's house, an unexpected guest should go away quietly.

There are other taboos and regulations concerning the homes of sericulturists, such as forbidding a stranger to enter the house, prohibitions on shouting, crying, and knocking doors or windows in the house. Liquor, vinegar, and anything smelling of fish or mutton should not be brought into a sericulturist's house and it is forbidden to dig the ground, cut grass, husk rice with a mortar and pestle or to burn fur and hair around a sericulturist's house. In the past, before putting silkworm eggs into a round shallow basket woven out of bamboo, people always pasted a wood engraving of a cat on the basket. This was because mice are natural enemies of silkworms. The mice often climbed to the shelves of silkworms and ate young silkworms when night-watchers dozed off. Hence, every household not only raises cats, but also retains the custom of pasting a picture of a cat on the basket.

Of course, some regulations are superstitious, for instance, menstruating women or women about to give birth are forbidden to raise silkworms; when buying mulberry leaves from other villages, in order to dispel evil spirits, sericulturists use mulberry branches to lash the leaves three times, and then feed them to silkworms. However, the purpose of all these prohibitions is to avoid noise pollution and bad smells. Young silkworms grow healthily in a clean and quiet environment.

When harvesting silkworm cocoons, sericulturists will, according to tradition, buy fish and meat, kill chickens and arrange feasts to celebrate. At this time, friends and relatives bring loquats, duck eggs and *zongzi* (a triangular dumpling made of glutinous rice wrapped in bamboo or other leaves) to visit these sericulturists. They come to send best wishes and ask how many *can hua* (harvests) these sericulturists get.

Can hua (literally "silkworm flower") is not a flower, but a word which indicates a good or bad harvest of silkworm cocoons. According to local custom, when young silkworms lie dormant for the fourth time, sericulturists will weigh these silkworms on a scale. For instance, if one catty of silkworms can spin out six catties of silkworm

47

48

48   Designs symbolizing good fortune decorate the kitchen.

49   Birthday celebration in a peasant's parlour. In rural homes south of the Yangtze River, as well as a bedroom and kitchen, there is also a parlour for receiving guests and eating meals. Wedding ceremonies and funerals are often held there.

49

47   Farmers in the villages north of the Yellow River sleep on a heated *kang* while beds are commonly used by farmers south of the Yellow River. Beds used by farmers south of the Yangtze River are exquisitely made.

50   Women sericulturists go to a temple to burn joss sticks to pray for an abundant harvest of silkworms.

51   The mulberry leaves for silkworms must be fresh and clean. Women go to the mulberry fields to collect the mulberry leaves every morning.

51

cocoons, the six–catty cocoons are called *liu fen can hua* (*liu* means six, and *fen* is a unit of measurement). The word *can hua* is often used in reference to the silkworm trade, but its meaning has various connotations according to the situation.

For example, local people call women sericulturists *can hua gu niang* (*gu niang* means a girl). On the morning of the first day of the lunar year, a woman sericulturist must, according to tradition, sweep the floor from the outside to the inside of a house. It is called *sao can hua di* (sweep the floor of *can hua*), meaning that there will be a good harvest of silkworm cocoons when *can hua* is swept into a house.

On New Year holidays, people will greet each other by saying, *gong xi fa cai* (may you make a fortune) and *can hua er she si fen*) (wish you a good harvest of silkworm cocoons).

On the day of the Qingming Festival, at the beginning of April, *can hua gu niang* will insert *can hua* in their hair at the temples. *Can hua* here refers to small flowers made of colourful paper and silk, or cocoons folded into the shape of a flower, or golden yellow vegetable flowers. The *can hua gu niang* will go to a monastery to pray together at an appointed time. They will also buy some silk flowers from the monastery and insert them in round shallow baskets. This is called *tao can hua* (*tao* here mean to beg). They believe that *can hua* coming from a monastery can expel all the evils in a sericulturist's house, so they will have a brisk silkworm business. At night, the woman of the house will prepare a delicious dinner. The family then gets together to drink. This is called *can hua jiu* (*jiu* means liquor). Drinking *can hua jiu* means that they will do their best to raise silkworms.

When a couple get married, the girl's parents will send the couple two young mulberries, two round shallow baskets of silkworms and silk clothes and bedding as a dowry. They hope that the bride will bring brisk business.

52

53

54

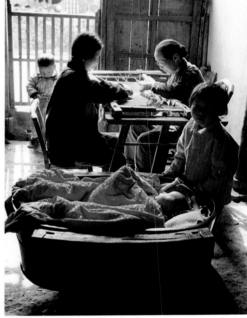

52 According to local tradition, women who raise silkworms wear flowers on their upswept hair, wishing to have an abundant harvest of silkworms.

53 The corner of a sericulturist's house.

54 A picture of a cat.

56

55 A picture of the Goddess of Silkworms.

56 Women do embroidery in their leisure time.

57   Some embroidery.

58   Middle-aged peasant women in Suzhou often wrap black kerchiefs on their heads.

58

Embroidery

The girls of Suzhou, Nantong, Wuxi, Changzhou, Yangzhou, Suqian and Dongtai in Jiangsu Province where silkworms are raised are renowned for their embroidery. Wuxian County of the city of Suzhou is the home of the famous Suzhou embroidery. When collecting folk stories in Suzhou I heard that the ancient custom of tattoo led to the development of the art of embroidery.

In antiquity, this region suffered from frequent floods. According to local legends, there was a flood dragon hiding in the water who often wrecked ships and killed people. Later, people found out that the flood dragon didn't harass other dragons. So they drew the heads and eyes of dragons on the sterns of their boats. They also cut their hair short, and draped their hair over their shoulders, and tattooed designs of dragons on their bodies in case they were killed by dragons when falling into the water. This is the origin of the ancient custom of shortening the hair and tattooing the body.

Three thousand years ago, the eldest son of King Zhou, Tai Bo, and his brother, Zhong Yong, moved to the region south of the Yangtze River in the early Zhou Dynasty leading many people in order to abdicate the throne in favour of their third brother. They brought advanced water management techniques to the Yangtze River valley. This led to the construction of canals and floods were diverted to Taihu Lake. Having no place to live, the flood dragons gradually became extinct. However, the custom of tattoo still prevailed. Tai Bo had already died by that time, and Zhong Yong decided to change the painful custom. One day, Zhong Yong and a few elders were discussing the matter

59 Village girls washing clothes beside a stream.

at home, while Zhong Yong's granddaughter Nu Hong was sewing. While sewing, she was listening carefully and pricked her finger on the needle. She hit upon an idea. If the patterns of flood dragons were embroidered on clothes, the tattoos could be replaced by the embroidery. Everyone thought this was a good idea.

Nu Hong stayed at home to do embroidery for seven days and nights. Eventually she finished a robe with a pattern of flood dragons on it. Zhong Yong put on the robe at once and went into the street. The people applauded the beautiful design. Consequently, other women did the same as Nu Hong. First they embroidered dragons and then flowers, grass, worms, and fish on the clothes. The more they did embroidery, the more beautiful and elaborate the embroidery became. In order to commemorate Nu Hong, doing embroidery is also called *nu hong* (needlework) even today.

This is merely a legend. However, according to historical records, embroidery originated in the Zhou Dynasty. At that time, after each autumn the king ordered government officials to wear embroidered robes and offer sacrifices to Heaven, to pray for an abundant harvest of all food crops. Before troops went to battle, the general leading the army had his name embroidered on the army flag. Military maps were embroidered since the third century.

Girls in the region start learning embroidery at the age of seven or eight. In the old society, the poor did embroidery for money in order to support their families. It was called *min jian xiu* (folk embroidery). The daughters of the rich also did embroidery for the beauty of it. They embroidered love tokens like pouches for their husbands and they also embroidered clothes, skirts and bedding. This was called *gui ge xiu* (boudoir embroidery). According to local custom the girl would receive a wooden shed decorated with embroidered cloth as her dowry on her wedding day. It is said that nobody wanted to marry a girl who could not embroider.

The clothing in the region is beautiful and unique. The village women in Wuxian all wear checkered kerchiefs trimmed with lace in blue, black and white on their heads and aprons with embroidered flowers. The skirt band tied at the waist emphasizes the figure of a slender girl, and the two white tassels of the skirt band sway rhythmically when she walks.

60 Huishan clay figurines from the city of Wuxi, in Jiangsu Province, and Taohuawu woodcuts and *Pingtan* (storytelling and ballad singing in Suzhou dialect) from Suzhou are all popular traditional folk arts.
The smiling babies sculpted in clay by Huishan artists are considered a symbol of family harmony.

61 An early Taohuawu woodcut depicts a happy scene of women in the Qing Dynasty.

Legend has it that the clothing originated 2,400 years ago. At that time, the region in Jiangsu and Zhejiang provinces belonged to the principality of Wu of the Zhou Dynasty. One day, Xi Shi, a consort of the prince of Wu, went to Taihu Lake to admire the lotuses. She saw a girl collecting lotuses who had paused to sit on a small boat. With lotus leaves on her head and lotus flowers dotted on her skirt, the girl looked charming. After returning to the palace, Xi Shi began copying the girl's dress with colourful silk. Before long, a clothing decoration called *qing lian bao tou he hua dou* (turban with lotus motif) was passed on from the palace among the people and handed down through generations.

However, the dress of women in the lake region is also practical as well as beautiful. They often get up to work before dawn. Because it is cool in the morning, it is warmer with a scarf wrapped around the head. Wearing a close-fitting jacket with narrow sleeves, a woman always looks neat and it is good for working. When mowing wheat and threshing the rice paddy, the wheat and rice will not fall on her clothing, so she can avoid being pricked by the grain thorns.

The apron has many uses. It helps shield against wind and cold while washing vegetables or clothes at the banks of a river, thus preventing waist pains. When cooking, washing and working in the fields, the apron helps keep clothes tidy.

小廣寒

時請妙齡中清容吳倍唎會唱

62 *Pingtan* is often played to a full
house.

63 A picture of a *Pingtan*
performance engraved in a
Taohuawu woodcut of the early
period of this century shows that
performances then were similar to
those of today.

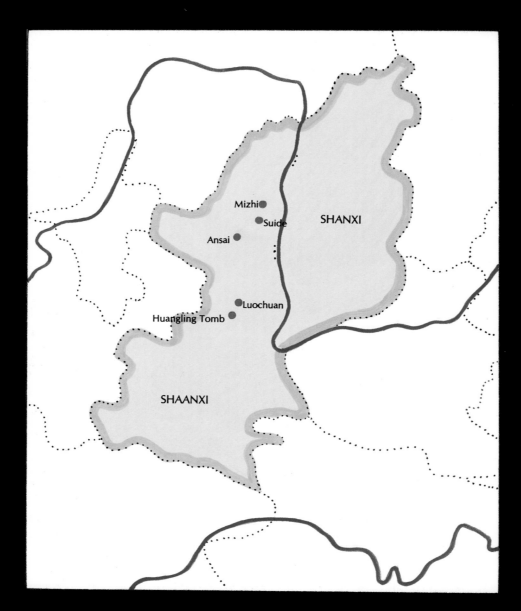

III. Loess Plateau

I came to the Loess Plateau in Shaanxi and Shanxi provinces to collect folk stories one winter. It is one of the biggest loess plateaus in the world. The ground is covered with golden loess and innumerable gullies cut by running water. Among the gullies stand round hills, long strips of mountain ridges and 1,000-to 2,000-metre-high *yuan* (a special kind of topography seen on the Loess Plateau) with a flat top. With countless mountains and gullies the Loess Plateau contrasts sharply with the lake region south of the Yangtze River.

The Loess Plateau is the cradle of the Chinese nation. Legend has it that 5,000 years ago the Yellow Emperor (Xuan Yuan), leader of the Huaxia tribe (an ancient name for the Chinese), invented the boat and horse–drawn carriages, the palace and the *zhinanche*, which was an ancient Chinese horse–drawn cart with a wooden stick which functioned as a compass as it always pointed to the south. He also ordered his officials to formulate a written language, and to make musical instruments. The Yellow Emperor was therefore called the "ancestor of human civilization" by later generations. His tomb is located in Huangling County in the north of Shaanxi Province. First of all I went to the town of Suide, an important military base in the border areas 2,000 years ago. Under the order of Emperor Qin Shi Huang, the general, Meng Tian of the Qin Dynasty, directed the building of the Great Wall here.

Cave Dwellers

Wangjiajian is a village with only some one hundred households. The sun shone into the courtyards and cave dwellings at the banks of the streams. On the bare branches of date trees in the courtyards hung golden corncobs, and a chain of red peppers was suspended across the doors. Chickens were eating and clacking paying no attention to me.

I was warmly received by the family of a villager named Wang Shuhou. The host, a white towel tied on his head and an old fur–lined jacket draped over his shoulders, took my luggage for me. His wife drew aside the blue cotton curtain and took me into their cave dwelling and invited me to sit on their *kang* (a heated brick bed).

It is usual for a host to invite guests to sit on a *kang* in the villages of North China. A *kang* is the centre of activity in rural homes. The *kang* becomes a bed when a quilt and mattress are unfolded on it. When the bedding is removed and tables are put on it, the *kang* is the dining area. Later the children do their homework on their *kang* and women do their needlework there. Guests are also received on the *kang*. The wall beside the *kang* is painted with all kinds of flower designs and historical stories. This is called *kangweihua* (painting around the *kang*).

The hollow *kang* made of adobe or stone is connected with the cooking stove. Through a pipe at the bottom of the *kang*, smoke rises from the chimney on the top

64   Farmland and a flock of sheep on the Loess Plateau.

65   Gullies and ravines have formed because of erosion.

64

65

of the cave dwelling. This heating method not only saves firewood, but keeps the air of the cave dwelling fresh as well.

However, babies may sometimes climb up to the top of the kitchen range from the *kang* and the cooking pot may endanger their lives. So, a pot lid with a heavy stone plate is used, so that the child cannot remove the lid. In regions without stone plates, people set up *kangweizi* which are wooden rail fences beside the kitchen range.

As soon as I sat on the *kang*, the hostess laid a table in the centre of the *kang* and brought in several dishes of apples, peanuts and liquor-saturated dates. She told me these foods were produced by the village. The dates are made by cleaning and drying fresh dates, then putting them into a jar, and then finally sprinkling a bit of white spirits into the jar. Two weeks later, the dates are fermented and sweet and aromatic. It is said that such dates can invigorate the function of the spleen and are beneficial to the kidney.

The large, sweet red dates of northern Shaanxi Province are widely renowned. Farmers usually plant several date trees in front of and behind their cave dwellings. Each autumn they dry one or two sacks of dates for guests and friends and to use for coaxing children and steamed buns. On New Year's Day, birthdays, and at weddings and other festivals, people are often presented with a pagoda-shaped steamed cake with dates. On the morning of New Year's Day, every household makes *zaochuanchuan*, a chain of dates with golden cornstalks and red dates, and hang them around babies' necks as festival decorations.

In winter, farmers often make simple dishes, such as boiled Chinese cabbage and carrots with mutton. However, they spend much time making staple foods. There are some dozen staple foods.. Besides the common *laofan* (strained boiled millet which is then steamed), steamed cakes and noodles, there are two special local foods: *getuo* and *qianqianfan*. *Qianqianfan* is a kind of thin gruel made of ground soybeans, cow peas, corn and millet. To make a *getuo*, put a small piece of kneaded dough on the palm of the left hand, press and then push the dough with the thumb of the right hand, finally put the curled flour slices into the pot and the *getuo* is finished. Of course people eat *jiaozi* (dumplings with meat and vegetable stuffing) on festivals or when having guests.

There are three ways to make noodles here. A rolling pin is used to roll the dough till it becomes thin, and then it is cut into thin slices known as *qiemian*; use two hands to draw a dough till it becomes a very thin strand called *latiaozi*; press the doughs with a tool called *helechuangzi* into round and thick strips and these are called *helemian*.

I had already heard that eating *helemian* is very convenient and helps to resist hunger, so when our hostess asked me what I wanted for lunch, I said that I would like to eat *helemian*. So, she began mixing the flour with water, and the host brought in a *helechuangzi* and set it on the kitchen range. A *helechuangzi* is a wooden vessel with a perforated copper plate at the bottom. He filled the bottom with the dough, pushed it with a wooden staff, and the noodles were pressed out from the small holes. When the noodles reach a certain length, they are cut with a knife and they will fall into the pot. The noodles are ladled out when they are ready. The noodles are seasoned with sesame, onion pieces, sliced carrots, sesame oil, soy sauce and vinegar, etc. Hot and fragrant, they taste delicious.

After lunch, I surveyed the cave dwelling at which I stayed. It was about seven metres long and three and a half metres wide and high. The cave dwelling was very brightly lit. The window was as high as the top of the cave dwelling and beside the window was the heated *kang*. Furniture, pots and pans stood against the wall. The cave was cosy and comfortable.

Cave dwellings are widely distributed along the middle and upper reaches of the

67

66 The Yellow River flowing through the Loess Plateau.

66

Yellow River and have been the homes for many generations on the Loess Plateau. This region covers an area of 600,000 square kilometres and is inhabited by 40 million people. The cave dwellings preserve heat because of a solid and thick roof, so they are warm in winter and cool in summer. They are easy to build at a cheap cost. They are built around mountains and are good for the environment because they don't occupy any arable land or destroy any landscapes. They also help to protect the ecological environment and have drawn the attention of international architects. In northern Shaanxi, not only do people live in cave dwellings, but wells, livestock pens, vegetable plots, toilets and all kinds of facilities are also constructed in the cave dwellings. The farmers have built caves in which vegetables can be planted in winter. They pull up Chinese cabbages with the roots. After the main roots are cut off, the cabbages are planted in caves with no sunshine. The Chinese cabbages can survive because, though a drop of water turns to ice immediately outside the caves, the vegetables do not freeze and do not go bad because of the higher soil temperature inside the caves. Therefore, farmers can eat green Chinese cabbage in winter as well as in other seasons.

67

The cave dwellings are usually dug in winter. People often choose a place beside cliffs and without gullies but with solid soil, a southern exposure, a leeward side, convenient communications and easy access to water and where there are no floods to built their cave dwellings. There are two kinds of cave dwellings. A cave dwelling near a cliff with windows is called *Tuyao* (earth cave dwelling). Another is built by excavating an earth model the same size as the future cave dwelling, and then the cave dwelling is built with stones and bricks, and finally the earth model is removed and filled with two or three metres of earth which is pressed down.

67 People live in cave dwellings surrounded by mountains.

68 Rural courtyards undulate with the rise and fall of the landscape.

69 Schooling is also held in cave dwellings.

69

68

69

70

71

70   Inside a cave dwelling.

71   A corner of a kitchen inside a cave dwelling: a niche in the wall, an ancient lamp, vegetables produced locally.

It is called *shiyao* (stone cave dwelling) or *zhuanyao* (brick cave dwelling).

On the third day when I arrived at Wangjiajian, we came across a happy occasion —the closure of a stone cave's *helongkou*. A *helongkou* is a breach left in the central section of the top of a cave dwelling. As long as the breach is covered with a *helongshi* (a stone for the closure of the breach), the new cave dwelling is considered completed. In the past, people were superstitious and afraid that evil spirits would enter the new buildings. So they put the hearts of three small animals (rooster, rabbit and wild pheasant) into a small hole dug on the *helongshi* beforehand as sacrifices to the gods, to get rid of evil spirits and keep the people safe.

Many things were hung beside the *helongshi*: a pair of red chopsticks, a writing brush, a Chinese ink slab, an almanac, a red bag containing wheat, millet, sorghum, corn and broom corn millet, colourful strips of cloth, and colourful silk threads. All these represented their hopes, which were to have good luck, good harvests and happy life.

Noon is the time to close the breach. An old stonemason and the host climbed to the top of the cave dwelling, laid the *helongshi* into the breach and hung chopsticks and other things on the stone. "The breach is closed!" exclaimed the villagers. Firecrackers began crackling and spluttering. The host threw cakes, coins, sewing kits and food to the crowd. It is said that those who get coins will make fortunes and girls who get a sewing kit will become embroidery experts.

71

72   *Helemian* (noodles) is the most common meal in northern Shaanxi Province. Put the wooden *helechuangzi* (a kind of tool for making *helemian*) on the kitchen range and press the *helemian* into boiling water in a pan till it is ready for the table.

73

72

73 Donkeys are the main
livestock in northern Shaanxi
Province. They are used for
transporting grain and coal and
pulling stone mills and people ride
them to get around.

74

75

74   When a stonemason places a *helongshi* (a stone to close the breach) into the breach on the top of a cave dwelling, the new cave dwelling is considered to be fully completed. According to tradition, the host will hold a celebration for the completion of the home.

75   The antithetical couplets and some things which symbolize good fortune are prepared for the celebration.

Wedding Customs in Northern Shaanxi

A young man named Wang Mingzhong in the village was going to get married. He set up a shed as a temporary kitchen in his courtyard. People came in and out. Some were busy killing pigs or sheep, some were making cakes or steamed buns and some

76

were making papercuts.

All preparations were being done in an orderly way. A list of the jobs was posted on the wall—a person in overall charge, cooks, accountants, and those responsible for receiving guests, preparing wine, carrying and heating water, odd jobs, etc. They were all Wang's neighbours. They were happy to help Wang and to come and add to the fun.

At dawn, a band started out to escort the bride to the wedding. According to tradition, they brought the dowry and two long cakes made of glutinous millet. When the woman's family accepted the two cakes, it meant that the woman would leave her mother. So the cakes were also called *limugao* (cakes for leaving mother). The bride daubed her face with ashes. It was said making herself ungainly with ashes could prevent her from being taken away by evil spirits on her way to the wedding. Of course, no one believes there are evil spirits today and the bride doesn't daub her face nowadays.

77

76   The procession to welcome
the bride on the way to the village.

77   In accordance with traditional
wedding ceremonies, after
entering the bridegroom's home,
the bride as well as the bridegroom
must kowtow to their ancestors
and parents, then the bride and
bridegroom kowtow to each other
and go into the bridal chamber.

78 Friends and relatives taking part in the wedding ceremony place their gifts on the table. Among the gifts are pairs of coins, clothes, and cakes.

When the group came back to the village, firecrackers were set off and the band started playing music. After they entered the door of the house, according to tradition, they made kowtows to Heaven and their parents and they carried a rice container as a symbol for good crops into the bridal chamber. On the rice container was a mirror, a scale and a ruler. It is said that the mirror detected demons and the scale and ruler had the function of hoping that the new couple would be upright, besides getting rid of evil spirits and wishing the couple a peaceful and happy life.

After the bride entered the bridal chamber, she first washed her face and combed her hair. These were adapted from the ancient customs of *kailian* and *jiaji*. The former means to pluck the fine hair off the bride's face with a silk thread; the latter means that the girl should do her hair in a bun and insert it with a pin. When the bride was ready, her mother-in-law brought a bowl of *jiaozi*. While the bride was eating *jiaozi*, her mother-in-law asked a question with a double meaning, "Shengma?" (*sheng* means "not mature" or "give birth" in Chinese; *ma* is a word indicating a question.) The shy bride answered yes. So the mother-in-law smiled with satisfaction: the daughter-in-law would like to have a healthy grandchild for her.

In Luochuan County, people put four small plates covered with bowls on a serving tray. The four plates contain coins, salt, wheat bran, and fried dough and the bride is asked to open the bowls. If she opens the plate containing coins, it means that the bride will be industrious and thrifty in running a home and can make money in the future; if she opens the plate with wheat bran (*maifu*), it is a sign that she will have a baby, because bran and happiness are homophonic in Chinese; if she opens the plate with salt, it means that husband and wife will live happily to a ripe old age. The worst thing is if she opens the plate with fried dough, because the fried dough symbols greed. However, the bride will get a hint before opening the plates. Therefore, no brides ever open the plate containing fried dough.

At night, people begin teasing the bride in the bridal chamber. Everyone can take part in the activity except her parents-in-law and her married brothers. All kinds of tricks are played on the bride and groom, so laughter can be heard in the bridal chamber.

The custom of teasing the bride has a reason behind it. In the past, the bride and bridegroom didn't know each other because of the system of arranged marriage until the day they got married. Teasing the bride helped to dispel shyness between the newly-acquainted couple. Now for the couple who arrange their own wedding, teasing the bride not only adds to the happy atmosphere of the wedding, but promotes friendship among the relatives as well.

The day following the wedding, the couple will visit the bride's family to thank the friends and relatives with gifts. As soon as the groom enters the house, his sister-in-law who is behind the door throws cooking ashes on his face; when he eats *jiaozi*, he will find that the stuffing is made of ground pepper and pod shells. This is a way to tease the new member of the family and create a good atmosphere.

77

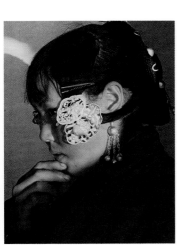

79

79 A bride.

80

80   The women of the village
want to see the bride. Since they
are shy to enter the bridal
chamber, they have to peep at the
bride from the window.

81   Birth, death and marriage are considered as three important events in life. Every place has its own traditions in connection with these. A baby turns one month old so the women are busy preparing food for guests. The grandmothers are showing the gifts presented to the baby by the guests.

82   A post-funeral feast.

82

81

Papercuts and *Mianhua*

In Shanxi and Shaanxi provinces, almost every home is decorated with papercuts on the windows and doors.

Papercuts are a handicraft made by women. They use scissors and paper to cut all kinds of pictures such as pomegranates, lotuses, peach blossoms, mice, fighting roosters and rabbits eating carrots.

To get rid of the old and make way for the new, every household puts up papercuts on the newly plastered window paper on the eve of Spring Festival. Chinese farmers still have the tradition of arranging farm production according to the lunar calendar. They number the years with twelve symbolic animals: the rat, ox, tiger, rabbit, dragon, snake, horse, sheep, monkey, rooster, dog and boar. So the papercuts of the twelve animals are indispensable. The papercut of an animal pasted on doors, windows and cupboards must correspond to the year of that animal according to the lunar calendar. Papercuts are done all over China, but are different in the method in different areas.

Jiangsu and Zhejiang provinces in the lower reaches of the Yangtze River have a humid and rainy climate. People don't use papercuts to decorate windows, they use them to decorate embroidery and lanterns instead. Besides using scissors, a special knife is also used to carefully cut and trim the paper, showing the splendid scenery south of the Yangtze with smooth lines.

83   A woman making papercuts.

There is scanty rain and a dry climate in North China. To make the papercuts durable and wind-resistant, women often cut thick lines.

The papercuts in Shanxi and Shaanxi provinces are part of the local customs of the Loess Plateau. When a woman is going to have a baby, her mother-in-law will paste a papercut of a tiger on the door, to signify that when the tiger guards the door, devils dare not enter the house to make mischief and that the baby will grow up healthily. When harvest time comes, if it is cloudy and drizzling for days on end, farm women will make several papercuts of people holding brooms and hang them on the door and branches of trees. The paper figures can presumably sweep away the black clouds, so the sun may come out to dry the wheat.

Nowadays, the superstitions concerning the papercuts have been toned down. However, women still decorate cave dwellings with all kinds of papercuts just for their beauty and not to dispel spirits. It is said that a boy often chooses a girl who is good at doing papercuts and embroidery. So you can often see there girls around seven and eight years old in a circle absorbed in learning to do papercuts.

84

84   Window, the edge of the *kang* and cupboards inside cave dwellings are all decorated with papercuts.

Mianhua is art created with flour. Fermented flour is kneaded into various shapes such as animals, gourds, fruits and flowers, and then steamed and finally coloured.

In Mizhi County of Shaanxi Province, I was fascinated as an old woman kneaded the flour. She cut a small piece of dough and rubbed it several times. First she made a body of a bird. Then she rubbed a small piece of dough into short noodles, pressed them flat, pasted them on the back of the bird and made the wing of the bird with a comb. Finally she made the beak. She had kneaded a singing skylark.

It was even more interesting to see her knead a monkey. She kneaded the flour into

82

85

85   The *hua* (flower) cakes in northern Shaanxi, also called *li* (courtesy) cakes, are made in the form of a tiger. The tiger was originally the totem of a tiger-worshipping clan when there was a slave society. Later it developed into a mascot to dispel evil. Therefore, tiger-shaped cakes are given to new parents, at weddings or to those building a new house. This tiger-shaped cake is a wedding present.

86   Cakes baked in the shape of people presented to a one-month-old baby.

86

a monkey with a hat very quickly. Finally, she put two black pieces of millet on the head of the monkey for the eyes. I calculated the time she took to make the dough sculptures: four minutes for the skylark and six minutes for the monkey.

When asked the origin of *mianhua*, she did not know. She said that it was handed down from generation to generation. Research says *mianhua* was related to the customs of funeral and sacrificial rites. Three thousand years ago in the Shang Dynasty, slaves were buried alive with their dead masters. Wooden and pottery figurines were buried with feudal lords in feudal society. Later, simple dough figurines were buried with the dead masters instead. Nowadays, when paying respects during the festival for the dead, the Qingming Festival, people in northern Shaanxi Province still keep the ancient customs of watering the graveyard and offering *mianhua* as sacrifices to ancestors.

Today *mianhua* is used as a gift. In the home of a person who just got married, we saw *mianhua* which were sent by his relatives as a congratulatory gift, each weighing two kilogrammes. The *mianhua* with a picture of dragons and phoenixes was called *long feng cheng xiang* (dragons and phoenixes show prosperity). The *mianhua* in the shape of a chain of locks expresses the hope that the newly married couple will live to an old age happily. Eighteen pairs of *mianhua* sent by eighteen relatives were arranged together just like an art display of *mianhua*.

According to a local custom, when returning to her parents' home, a married woman must bring half a basket of *mianhua* with her. The ring–shaped *mianhua* presented to her parents and other elders expresses the wish that the elders should have a long life as the ring goes round without end. The *mianhua* are decorated with a bat and a sika deer as a symbol for the hope that the couple can spend their remaining years in happiness because the word for bat and happiness are homophonic in China. The word for sika deer and payment is also homophonic.

Mianhua shaped like a rabbit and tiger are given to children, to show the wish that a boy should be as strong as a tiger and a girl as lovely and clever as a white rabbit. *Mianhua* in the shape of birds is used to show that children will be good at singing and dancing like birds.

83

87   Embroidered tiger-headed shoes and pillows made of silk and satin.

87

88

88   A wall hanging in the shape of a tiger's head as a decoration and a mascot to dispel evil.

89   Clay toys.

90   When doing household chores, a woman often puts her baby on a *kang*. To prevent the baby from falling off the *kang*, the woman ties one end of a rope to the baby and the other end to a lion–shaped stone. This kind of stone sculpture is called a *Shuan Wa Shi* (stone for fastening a baby).

84

89

91   The paintings of the Loess
Plateau reflect the local life. The
painting of *Festival Celebration* is a
scene of the *yangge* dance,
land–boats, lion dances and
running donkeys.

91

Yangge and Waist Drum Dance

During the slack season in winter, young people in villages in northern Shaanxi begin doing the *yangge* dance and waist drum dancing in order to greet Spring Festival (first day of the first lunar month) and Lantern Festival (15th of the first lunar month).

On the lunar New Year's Day, after eating *jiaozi*, the *yangge* group begins paying New Year calls to the households. They wish the hosts a happy New Year and do the *yangge* dance in the courtyards. Accompanied by drums, they wave red silk waist bands. The hosts set off firecrackers to welcome the dancers' arrival and invite them to taste their home-made rice wine. The sounds of songs, drums and firecrackers blend, creating a festive atmosphere in the village. *Yangge* originated 2,000 years ago, as a religious activity to greet gods and dispel evil, but now it is a recreational activity in the sowing season or on holidays.

The most interesting part is waist drum dancing. A dancer with a red drum tied to his waist holds a drumstick with red silk, beating the drum while dancing. The rhythmical drum sound and graceful dance show the straightforward and uninhibited character of villagers in northern Shaanxi Province and is an expression of their happy and passionate feelings.

Ansai waist drum dancing and Luochuan waist drum dancing in northern Shaanxi have distinctive features. Ansai dancing includes vigorous movements accompanied by rhythmic drumbeats. At the climax of the dance, dancers beat drums while jumping into the air, uttering the sound "Haihai" excitedly. Luochuan dancing is done with a drum as big as a washbasin and the drumstick is long and thin. The dancers wear white war gowns, with a towel tied on their heads and flags on their backs. Their costumes are decorated with the designs of ancient bronze wares. They dance back and forth, jumping from time to time, to the drums just like soldiers fighting each other.

Decayed wooden drums covered with boa skins were unearthed from the Yin ruins of Anyang City, Henan Province, which implies that drums appeared more than 3,000 years ago. In ancient times, drums were used to offer sacrifices, fight the enemy, sound alarms, and give the time, as well as for daily recreational activities.

As for the origin of the waist drum in north Shaanxi Province it is thought that it was a tool for officers in ancient times and for soldiers stationed at borders to sound alarms and train troops. Especially for cavalries, the drums accompanied the rhythm of the horse's hooves, as the soldiers yelled and advanced. Later, the waist drums were handed down among the people by demobilized soldiers. This was deduced from the fact that the waist drums in northern Shaanxi are popular in the frontier fortress regions near the ancient Great Wall and that dancers dress in the clothing of ancient warriors and the dances have martial elements and formations similar to those of ancient times. Another view of the origin of the dance is that shepherds in northern Shaanxi Province were the earliest makers of the waist drums. They beat drums made with sheepskin to liven up their lonely life. Later, beating drums, along with other percussion instruments, gradually became a recreational activity for villagers to pray for favourable weather for crops and a happy life.

87

92 On holidays or at the Chinese New Year, an amateur village troupe performs local opera. Though the performers are all farmers and the sets, props and costumes are very simple, the spectators enjoy the performances.

93   Villagers rehearsing the waist–drum dance at the foot of the Great Wall.

94   Legend has it that the Wei Feng Gong and Drum Dance has a history of more than 4,000 years. Gongs and drums are played simultaneously and sometimes the number of performers may reach several hundred. The imposing scene is full of grandeur with great momentum, hence the name Wei Feng (which means power and grandeur) Gong and Drum Dance.

95   The *Bie* Drum originated in wars of ancient times, therefore performers wear copies of the costumes of ancient warriors.

96   Nine meandering lantern lines at the night of the Lantern Festival in Yan'an in northern Shaanxi Province. The tradition of *Zhuanjiuqu* (walking in nine meandering lines) is continued in some cities and towns on the night of the Lantern Festival in North China, in which 361 poles are set up in the square in advance, each 1.5 metres high. All kinds of lanterns are put on top of the poles. There is more than one metre between each pole. Ropes are used to separate the square into twisted passageways with only one entrance and one exit. On the night of the Lantern Festival, people come to appreciate lanterns and guess riddles. Because the passageways twist and turn with only one exit, only after a good deal of bother can people find the exit.

96

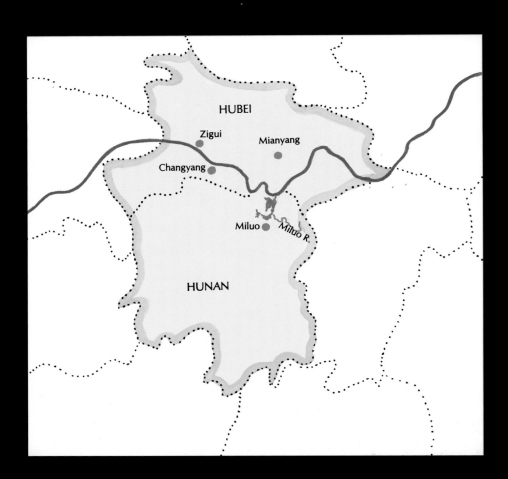

IV. Customs Handed Down from the State of Chu

THE fifth day of the fifth month of the lunar calendar is the Dragon Boat Festival. On this day, people put Chinese mugwort on their gates and burn incense in their homes, and eat *zongzi*, a triangular dumpling made of glutinous rice wrapped in leaves with sugar, and a dragon boat race is held. The Dragon Boat Festival is one of China's traditional festivals. A legend from ancient times said that this day was for offering sacrifices to the dragon—the ancestor of the Chinese nation. But in fact, 2,200 years ago this day was connected with the commemoration of Qu Yuan (340–278 B.C.), a poet of the State of Chu. Present-day Hubei and Hunan provinces were part of the State of Chu. Zigui County in Hubei is Qu Yuan's hometown and the Miluo River in Hunan Province is the river where Qu Yuan drowned himself. So during the Dragon Boat Festival, I arranged special trips to these two provinces to collect materials.

Dragon Boat Festival in the Miluo River Valley

In the early summer, the wheat is threshed in the Miluo River area. At this time rice has usually been tilled twice. So the peasants are not busy with farming. When I went to Quzici from Miluo County town, I saw many young women going back to their hometowns to see their parents with their husbands. They brought a lot of gifts. It is a custom in this area to bring *zongzi*, steamed dumplings, pork, dried cuttlefish and wine to their parents. They also bring palm-leaf fans because after the Dragon Boat Festival the weather will get hot, so the parents can use the fans to cool themselves.

The name of Quzici (Qu Yuan Temple) Village comes from the Qu Yuan Temple in the Yusi Mountains east of the village. Qu Yuan was a minister of the State of Chu who advocated reforms and to ally with the State of Qi to fight with the State of Qin. But the king of Chu believed some slander against Qu Yuan. The king not only refused to adopt Qu Yuan's advice, but also exiled him to the border area near the Miluo River. During the 15 years of exile he wrote *Li Sao* (*The Lament*), *The Nine Odes* and *The Elegies* and other works to express his concern about the country and the people. In 278 B.C. the Qin troops stormed into the capital of Chu. When Qu Yuan heard the news he was filled with grief and indignation and drowned himself in the Miluo River.

When they heard the sad news of Qu Yuan's death, people who lived along the river rushed to the river with their boats to take Qu Yuan's body out of the river. At the same time, they threw *zongzi* into the river to feed the fish and shrimps, so that they would not devour Qu Yuan's body. This is the background of the legend of the Dragon Boat Festival.

Before Qu Yuan's death people already had this custom. Some folklore experts believed that the dragon boat race on the fifth day of the fifth lunar month was a religious activity of the ancients for driving away the god of plagues and the devils. But the famous modern scholar, Wen Yiduo (1899–1946), said that the fifth day of the fifth

97

98

97   Situated south of the middle reaches of the Yangtze River, Hunan Province is located south of Dongting Lake, hence the name Hunan (South of the Lake). Most regions in the province are hilly and mountainous. Small basins scattered in the hills are rich and populous farming areas, which is shown by the picture.

98   Most towns in Hunan and Hubei provinces are located at the foot of mountains and beside streams. The picture was taken at Fenghuang County beside the Tuojiang River, west of Hunan Province.

99   Old-style streets and buildings in Fenghuang County.

100   Temples, ancestral halls and yamen (a governmental office in old China) built one or two centuries ago can be found inside and outside the town of Fenghuang. This is an ancient stage in the county, the door below it leading to an ancestral hall.

97

99

100

lunar month was the day for the people of the State of Wu and the State of Yue south of the Yangtze River to offer sacrifices to dragons because they called themselves the descendants of the dragon. Usually they cut their hair and tattooed dragon designs on their arms. On the fifth day of the fifth month they would paddle their dugout canoe with the design of a dragon on and throw some wrapped in tree leaves or in bamboo tubes into the water to offer sacrifices to dragons. Then finally they had a boat race.

Activities, such as rowing dragon boats and throwing *zongzi* into the river, were popular first in the areas of Chu. Then they spread to some other places.

The fifth day of the fifth lunar month was officially decided as the date for the Dragon Boat Festival by the imperial government of the Song Dynasty (A.D. 960–1279) to praise Qu Yuan's unyielding integrity.

In the early morning of that day the custom is to pick Chinese mugwort wet with dew, which is the custom everywhere. Young men and women of the villages go to the fields to cut mugwort, calamus and rattan and put them in front of the gates, which look green and fresh and have a delicate fragrance. The origin of the legend varies in different places. In Miluo County, the mugwort signifies horses; the long and straight calami look like bronze swords, and the rattan represents magic rope to tie up monsters and ghosts. When you put these things in front of the gates, it seems Zhong Kui, the hero who catches monsters, stands in front of the gate riding on a horse with a sword and rope in his hand, so that monsters will go away. Some people write the Buddhist tenet, "On the fifth day of the fifth lunar month, the Taoist master riding a mugwort tiger with calamus sword in hand so that mosquitoes and insects will go away," on paper and pasted it on the doors.

May was considered as evil by the ancients because the weather in May led to seasonal febrile diseases. Mosquitoes and flies breed quickly at this time and vipers, scorpions, centipedes, geckos and poisonous spiders also begin to come out at this time. In dealing with these diseases and poisonous insects, women draw the five poisonous creatures and put them on the wall and then prick them with needles. Or sometimes, women embroider the design of a tiger attacking the five poisonous creatures on their children's clothing to represent elimination of the five poisonous creatures. In ancient times the medical effects of the moxa were discovered. The moxa roll made of dried mugwort leaves can cure extravasated blood and swelling and inflammation through moxibustion. If mugwort is decocted and drunk it can stop bleeding, and cure dysentery and gynecological problems. The smell of the mugwort can drive mosquitoes and flies away. So it is put on the doors to drive away mosquitoes, flies and other insects. The root of the calamus, which grows beside the water, can ease pain and is good for the stomach and urinary bladder. In ancient times it was steeped in wine to make the wine more tasty.

98

101   An ancient ferrying method is still used at some fords in Hunan and Hubei provinces: The boatman stands aft and steers the ferry by pulling on an iron or rattan cord spanning the river.

102   Stores and stands selling chilli can be seen everywhere in the streets of southwest China, whose inhabitants have a special preference for spicy dishes.

101

In addition, every family mixes realgar, white spirits and water together and then spreads the mixture on the floors of their bedrooms, living rooms, kitchens and stables with mugwort twigs. A long time ago, when the family got together on the fifth day of the fifth lunar month they would drink light realgar wine (not too much realgar, which is poisonous). The grandmother would write the word king on the forehead of the children with the realgar wine which was a symbol for the wish that the children would be healthy and strong.

So we can see that the customs mentioned above represent the desire of the people to prevent diseases in summer.

In some places south of the Yangtze River, on the fifth day of the fifth lunar month, people not only spread wine on the floors of their rooms and clean their houses, they

103

103   In the early morning of the Dragon Boat Festival, villagers return from the fields carrying their collection of dew-covered Chinese mugwort. They will not only plant the grass in their home but also take some to sell in the city.

104   Hanging calamus and mugwort by the door to banish evil spirits and expel insects.

104

105

105   For the Dragon Boat Festival, it is customary for children to wear red bibs or coats embroidered with the design "fierce tiger driving away the five poisonous insects."

106   Realgar wine is used to write the Chinese character *wang* (king) on the forehead of a child, in the hope that he will grow up as strong as a tiger, the king of all beasts.

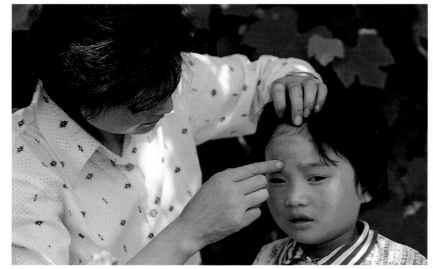

106

107

107   On the eve of the Dragon Boat Festival, housewives have their hands full making the festive delicacy *zongzi* for family consumption or for use as a festive gift.

108   The soaked glutinous rice is put in a cone–shaped reed leaf.

109   The reed leaf is wrapped in the shape of a quadrangle, which is then tied up by a cattail stem.

110   Now the *zongzi* is ready to be boiled in water.

108

also wash their dogs in ponds. Children cheer around the ponds.

The rich festival lunch starts with eating *zongzi* which is the custom everywhere in China. But the ingredients and flavours vary in different places. In Quizici Village, the *zongzi* is made of glutinous rice wrapped with reed leaves and boiled in soda ash water. They should be eaten while they are hot. That is the difference between eating *zongzi* in Quzici Village in Hubei Province and in Beijing. In Beijing, the *zongzi* is made of glutinous rice and dates and then put in cold water before being eaten.

The *zongzi* made in Jiaxing in Zhejiang Province is stuffed with ham. The glutinous rice is mixed with soy sauce and the ham is soaked with sugar, wine and salt. Then one piece of fat meat is put in between two pieces of lean meat. In this way the fat will be absorbed by the rice and it will not taste greasy.

Guangdong *zongzi* has a distinctive flavour and there are different fillings. One kind of *zongzi* is stuffed with diced chicken, diced duck, lean pork, egg yolk, mushroom and fine mung bean mash. The big ones can reach half a kilogramme and are wrapped with lotus leaves.

At first people put rice in a bamboo tube and then boiled it in water. Two thousand years ago people began to wrap the rice with various kinds of leaves. They were named by their different shapes and the fillings were also different, such as sugar, dates, chestnut, and pine nuts. The famous *zongzi* at that time were mugwort–flavoured *zongzi* which were made by soaking rice with the mugwort leaves and milk *zongzi* which was made by soaking rice with cheese for one night.

In addition to *zongzi*, people also eat other dishes, such as stewed bamboo shoots, pork and edible fungus soup, fried amaranth and fried eel slices. The two–coloured amaranth is an ordinary vegetable, but it is said that people who eat the amaranth on the fifth day of the fifth month will not have stomachaches that year. So everyone eats

103

109

110

amaranth that day. And in some places, people thought that eating river snail, sweetened garlic and spring onion on that day would make them clever and good at counting because the Chinese word for garlic is pronounced the same way as the word for counting and the pronunciation of onion is the same as that of the word for clever.

111   The reed leaf should be
removed before eating a *zongzi*.

111

But races are usually held in the afternoon. In Miluo County, before the boat race the sailors have to carry dragon heads to the temple to pay tribute to Qu Yuan, and this is called offering a sacrifice to the dragon head. When I arrived in the Quzici Temple, I saw sailors with a white towel on their heads and white clothes enter the temple holding their boat flag, and shouldering dragon heads while beating drums and gongs along with the sound of firecrackers. They put the dragon head on the sacrificial altar and then kowtowed to Qu Yuan's portrait. Then the master of the ceremony tied a piece of red silk on the dragon head and the sailors carried the dragon head to the riverside and jumped into the water to put the dragon head on the boat. It was said that only in this way could the boat race run smoothly and that the sailors would have good luck and be safe in the coming year after taking a bath in the river on the fifth day of the fifth month. When the white dragon boat team left the temple, the red dragon boat team, green dragon boat team and golden dragon boat team entered the temple consecutively.

The dragon boat is about 20 metres long and 1.5 metres wide. It is decorated with a wooden dragon head and at the same time, the body of the boat, oar and rudder are all painted with the design of dragon scales. From afar they really look like dragons.

The dragon boats are usually made of the wood of fir trees. When a new boat has been built a ceremony will be held to launch the boat. First the carpenter holds the sacrificial plate to wish the new boat might move as quick as the wind and an arrow.

105

112   Before the contest, a ceremony is held by the villagers to pay homage to the dragon boats. The rowers present wine and various offerings at the bow of their boat, praying that they will not have an accident during the contest and that they want to win the first prize.

112

Then the carpenter will spread the three cups of wine as a sacrificial offering to heaven, the land and the dragon head.

Before the race, both banks of the Miluo River were crowded with people. After the starting signal was fired from a pistol, various-coloured dragon boats leapt on the surface of the water as quick as arrows. The sailors, captains, drummers and gong players are selected by the villagers. The requirements are that they should be good at swimming, strong and cooperate well together.

The green dragon boat team surpassed all the other teams and won first place. There is a saying there: "We would rather leave our land uncultivated than lose the boat race."

As early as the Tang Dynasty (618–907) dragon boat races had spread to Japan, Korea, Viet Nam and some other countries in Southeast Asia. Today, international dragon boat tournaments attract more and more sailors from various countries.

113

114

113   Paying homage to the head of the dragon. The contestants take turns kowtowing to the head of their dragon boat which is placed on the table.

114   Having paid respects to the head of the dragon, the rowers put it on their boat. The contest is ready to start.

115   The dragon boat contest on the Miluo River.

116   The contestants are all sturdy and robust men picked from the villagers.

Qu Yuan's Hometown

I visited Yuepingli in Zigui County, which was Qu Yuan's hometown. Along the way were green hills and clear waters and I felt as though I were in a landscape painting. But people complained about the strenuousness of climbing the rugged mountain path.

Two people with bamboo baskets on their backs walked slowly in front of me. Bamboo baskets carried on the back are popular here because they can spare the hands to hold the branches of trees or rocks to avoid falling down.

Two women came from the opposite direction. The one in front was a young mother and a baby was sound asleep with its head tilted to one side in the basket, which is a special basket for babies. The girl behind had a vase-shaped bamboo basket on her back.

I arrived in Yuepingli which is situated in an open valley. Smoke rose slowly from the kitchen chimneys. I saw three or four girls washing clothes in the stream. Frogs croaked continuously in the newly planed rice field.

At noon on the second day of my arrival I suddenly heard the deafening sound of gongs and drums and the crack of fireworks. It turned out that a young woman from the village was going to get married.

I had never seen such a grand team. Carrying various pieces of furniture and household utensils in baskets on their backs many young men walked slowly and carefully.

They had to be very careful because it was considered unlucky if part of the dowry fell out or ran into the rocks. I followed them closely. When they got to a shady place they took a rest. As soon as the young men stopped they said, "We are tired, bride, please light cigarettes for us! We are hungry, give us something to eat!"

At first, the bride was too shy to do that and hid behind her companion. Then the young men shouted again, "If you don't light cigarettes for us we won't have enough energy to go forward. Then we won't arrive at the bridegroom's home before dark! If you don't give us candies to eat, we'll shake with hunger. It won't be our fault if the furniture runs into the rocks!" So hearing that the bride's companion hurriedly pulled the bride over to light cigarettes for the young men and give them candies to eat. Suddenly a burst of laughter was heard. It turned out that these young men were making fun of the bride. In this way, they could relax and put the bride at ease as well. The wedding ceremony was held in the living room with the Chinese characters of happiness pasted on the wall and hung with a red ball made of strips of silk. The couple saluted the guests, the parents and then each other. As soon as the master of the ceremony

117

118

117   In the mountain area of Chu, mothers carry their babies around in a basket on their back.

118   A wicker basket for holding grain can also serve as an outdoor cradle.

119   In imperial China, the authorities made a point of extolling "chaste" and "heroic" women, i.e., those who refused to remarry after their husband's death or those who died in defence of their honour. In Hunan, there are still some memorial archways built hundreds of years ago in honour of such women.

120   Zigui County in western Hubei is the hometown of the great poet Qu Yuan. A memorial archway and stone tablets have been set up in his honour at the county seat.

119

120

121 The ancient history of Qu Yuan's hometown is manifest in its folk customs and architecture. The picture shows an ancient building that serves as a primary school.

122 The bride's dowry —furniture, clothing, quilts and mattresses—is carried to the house of the bridegroom by a team of sturdy young men.

121

122

finished speaking, it was time to set off firecrackers and begin the music and the bride and bridegroom entered the bridal chamber. I heard shouting, "Quick! Quick! Hurry up! Hurry up!" Then I saw the bride and bridegroom rush into the room. The custom was that whoever enters the room first will manage the household affairs. This custom is totally different from other places where the bride and bridegroom will be guided by other people to their rooms.

In the area of Zigui, the funeral customs are also very unusual. In Changyang County facing Zigui County across the Yangtze River there is singing and dancing when there is a death. Upon my arrival in Ziqiu Village in Changyang County, people were talking, "Last night I heard the sound of the firelock (a gunlock which produces a charge). Tian Zhengui's mother died."

It is the custom in this area that when old people die, the family uses a firelock to convey the news to their fellow villagers. When the villagers hear the sound they will go to offer their condolences by singing and dancing. It is called a mourning dance.

After supper I went to Tian's house together with some villagers. I saw that the living room was ablaze with light and an unnailed coffin was put in the courtyard. The children in mourning dress stood in the funeral room to receive people who came to offer condolences.

The villagers came one after another. They bowed to the dead person and then comforted the family. After this procedure, they began to dance in couples. After a while, they were out of breath and streamed with sweat.

The only musical accompaniment for the mourning dance is a drum and the drummer also sings. They usually sing something about the life of the dead person and also historical stories or love stories. The drummer I saw in Tian's house was an 83-year-old man. Though his hair was white, he was strong and his voice was loud and clear. When he finished one section the other people would repeat the last sentence. The atmosphere was lively.

When they stopped singing I asked the old man, "Why do you sing and dance when people die?" He told me that when a person who is over sixty dies we say that he has died a natural death. It is considered a happy event. Offering condolences by dancing and singing can help relieve the sadness of the family. In the past there was another superstitious saying that a mourning dance could reduce the sins committed by the dead person before his death and help the soul of a deceased person rise to heaven.

The mourning dance originated from the "beating basin song" of 2,000 years ago. It was recorded in ancient books that when the wife of Zhuang Zi, a philosopher of the Warring States Period, died, another philosopher, Hui Zi, went to offer condolences. He saw Zhuang Zi sitting on the ground singing funeral songs while beating a basin to mourn his wife.

Recently, some scholars thought that the mourning dance is connected with wars in ancient times. Three thousand years ago, before soldiers went to the battlefield or after they came back from the battlefield they would dance to music. In this way, they would boost their morale, relax, and mourn the dead.

At dawn, the villagers stopped dancing and began to nail the coffin. And then the coffin was taken away to the burial place accompanied by firecrackers and the sound of the drum.

113

123   Riding in a sedan chair, the bride arrives at the village of her new home.

124   Neighbours sing and dance through the night to mourn for the dead and console the bereaved family.

123

124

The Customs of the Thousand Lakes Province

Hubei Province is so named because of its geographical position north of Dongting Lake (*hu* means lake and *bei* means north). In ancient times, this area was a wide expanse of marshland. Afterwards the Jianghan Plain with an area of 30,000 square kilometres was silted up by the water with mud from the Yangtze and Hanshui rivers. In this area, there are more than 1,000 lakes, hence Hubei Province is called the Thousand Lakes Province.

Nanzui Village in Miaoyang County juts out into the Paihu Lake. More than 20 farm houses have been built on a platform, only one metre higher than the water surface of the lake. The local people said that in the past when it rained several days continuously, the village would be submerged. When the Yangtze and Hanshui rivers flooded this area, it became a vast expanse of water. When the flood came the villagers would move their furniture and some other things up to the attic and then they left for other places taking with them food and clothing. Some people went fishing; some sought refuge with their relatives and friends; and some wandered to other places to sing for a living. They went back to their home till the flood went away.

They had to build straw sheds to live in. Sometime later, inspired by the arches of bridges "water gate houses" were created which means that when a house is built, a hole one metre high and one metre wide is left from the base of the back wall. When the construction of the house has been finished the hole is filled in with bricks. So when floods come the bricks are moved away and the water flows out through the hole. In this way the wall of the houses can be protected from the force of the flood. When the flood recedes the hole is filled again. Some houses have undergone floods dozens of times, but they are still in good shape.

Fishing boats were scattered all over the lakes and some fishermen standing on the front of the boats were casting nets and some others were catching fish with lampshade–shaped nets. The local people used different ways to catch fish and they have about 20 kinds of fishing nets. The biggest net is several hundred or sometimes nearly 1,000 square metres. It is lifted by a winch.

What interested me most was the trap made for the fish by the fishermen. The fishermen put tree stumps in the lakes and then fenced them in with a net. When fish go into the trap they cannot get out. Finally they have to swim into a bag at the end of the net.

There is a saying in this area, "The fish is the son of the Dragon King. Everyone can fish no matter who he is." So it has become an unwritten law that people can fish around lakes and rivers. But at the end of spring, fishing is forbidden because that is the time for fish to spawn. In addition, if several fishermen are fishing with the lampshade–shaped net at the same time, the one who sees the fish first should cast his net first. If he cannot catch the fish, the others can cast their nets. Otherwise the person who rushes to cast the net would be condemned by other fishermen and the fish he catches would be sent back to the person who saw the fish first.

Fishermen are loyal to their friends. When they meet in the lakes on their fishing trips, whether they know each other or not they are friendly. After fishing they put their boats together and then go to eat and drink on one boat. The host of the boat cooks the food for them. They often put rice, vegetables, condiments, fish and meat into one pot. After cooking they will be served into the bowls in the order they were put in the pot. The meat is fat, but not greasy. The oil of the meat goes to the fish, which makes the fish fresh and delicious. And the juice from the fish permeates the vegetables and rice, which gives them a special taste.

The lakes abound with lotuses. In early summer, the new lotuses bud and come out of the water, so the green water is dotted with white and pink flowers.

The history of the lotus in China can be traced back to very ancient times. Two lotus seeds were found together with a pot of carbonized grain in 1972 in the ruins of the New Stone Age, near Zhengzhou in Henan Province. These relics are more than 5,000 years old. These lotuses are uncultivated and they grow every year. Lotus seed picking areas are divided by the villages along the lakes and villagers built watch towers to survey the lotuses. Early autumn is the time to pick lotus seeds. The date for picking lotus seeds has to be decided by villagers and at the same time they donate money to buy pork because they will get together to eat on that morning. After eating they will go down to the lakes. The boats rowed by the men are in a line. Women cut the seedpod of the lotus seeds, and the old people break the pods with bamboo slips to take the seeds out.

When the sun sets, the villagers will call it a day and go to the watchtowers. They put the lotus seeds together and then distribute them to each household. After going back home, they are busy shelling and drying the lotus seeds.

In early winter when the water is low, people begin to dig lotus roots. Whoever wants to dig the lotus roots can go. It is a hard job to get the roots out of the mud. Lotuses usually grow in mud about one metre deep. So people have to stand in the mud, which makes it hard to move.

The peasants have experience in digging lotuses. When they pick lotuses, they go to the places where there are old lotus leaves, so they can find big ones there. Sometimes they pick up lotuses which are not too deep in the mud. For the deep ones they have to tramp the mud on one side and then the root of the lotus will come out more easily.

125

125　A view of the lake area in Hubei. Local inhabitants depend on the lake for their daily needs. They fish, rear ducks and geese and cultivate lotus in the lake, which is often more lucrative than farming.

126　A typical household in the lake area. A one–square–metre movable water gate is installed in every wall to allay the impetus of floods. Under the eaves, colour paintings depicting legends of ancient heroes serve as decorations.

127　The age–old practice of fishing using cormorants is still in use today.

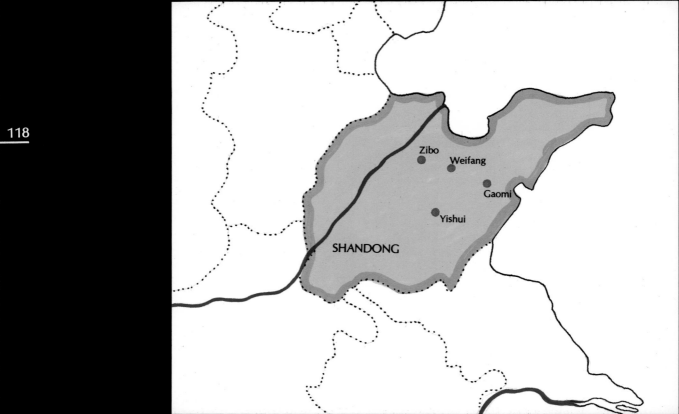

V. The Area of Qi and Lu

IT was in the fall that I went to visit Yishui County in the central part of the Yimeng Mountains in Shandong Province. The steep cliffs with flat tops reminded me of watchtowers, called *gu* by the locals. The area had already been inhabited as far back as 400,000 years ago. During the Warring States Period some 2,000 years ago, this land was part of the State of Lu. The remains of the wall that once divided the states of Qi and Lu can still be found at the Muling Pass on the Yi Mountain to the north of the county town. Covered with loess, sand and lime, the wall which stretched for hundreds of kilometres was built by the State of Qi, then the northern neighbour of the State of Lu. Today's Shandong Province, which once encompassed Qi and Lu, was later referred to as "the states of Qi and Lu."

The Wheelbarrow

On my way, a young man pushing a wheelbarrow passed by. Sitting on it was a pretty young woman dressed in a red flower-patterned jacket, dark-green pants and embroidered shoes. I learned they were newlyweds. The wife went back to her parents' home two days before and was supposed to return to her husband's home that day.

The wheelbarrow is a very popular and useful means of transportation in this mountain area. Every home owns at least one or two of them. Peasants here use wheelbarrows to carry corn, peanuts and sorghum stalks home from the fields and they also use it to carry fruit, vegetables and timber to sell at the market in town.

Two metres long and one metre wide, the barrow is made of a plank and a rubber wheel in the middle. The upper part of the wheel is higher than the board so as to lower the barrow's weight and make it run more smoothly. Under each shaft is a stand, making it easy to stop and to load and unload at any time. When pushing the barrow, a belt is tied on the shaft and put around the neck of the person pushing the barrow to share the heavy weight with the arms.

At the crowded country markets, barrows are used as counters on which grain, meat, vegetable and fruit are placed for sale. In the eyes of a stranger like me, this was like an exhibition of wheelbarrows. Light and mobile, it can run on both smooth roads and narrow and bumpy mountain paths and can carry as much as 300 kilogrammes.

Mountain Treasures in Yishui County and the Shandong Pancake

One day when we were driving to Niuchangzi Village, we stopped on the way to ask directions from a middle-aged woman drying peanuts on the threshing ground. When she learned we had come all the way from Beijing, she took a lot of peanuts up in her jacket and handed them to us through the car window. This proved the reputation

128   This level mountain top has been transformed into tracts of terraced fields.

129   In autumn, every village house in the Yimeng Mountains is surrounded by piles of newly harvested crops.

130   A light and handy means of transportation on narrow mountain paths, the wheelbarrow has been used by people of the Yimeng Mountains for generations.

128

129

that Shandong peasants have earned as being very hospitable.

When I arrived at Niuchangzi Village in the evening, Mr. Zhu invited me to stay with his family. When I entered his house, many dishes were already on the table. A chicken head sat in the bowl of diced chicken in brown sauce and was pointed right at me. One of the customs here require chicken heads be presented to guests. After sitting down, no one should eat until the guest has picked up the chicken head. During the dinner, the hostess brought in a dish that was wowed by everyone. I looked carefully and found it was fried scorpions. Though it was crispy and smelled good, I didn't dare touch it. When I was wondering how such a thing could be part of a famous cuisine, my host told me that it was from the Yimeng Mountains and was considered a famous Chinese delicacy. It was said to help prevent skin ulcers or scabies from developing if eaten frequently. Some people even said that it prevents cancer.

Scorpions thrive in the mountains of Yishui County. Every spring when people go to the mountains they turn over the rocks and pick out scorpions from stone cracks with bamboo clippers. They either sell them to Chinese pharmacists or boil them with salt before storing them in an oil jar. They only serve it when they have special guests visiting them.

After drinking three rounds of wine, the hostess brought in the Shandong pancake. Imitating people beside me, I spread out the pancake that had been folded into an oblong shape and wrapped in it green onion and Chinese toon sprouts. The fresh onion and the tasty Chinese toon sprouts make the crispy pancake very delicious.

Pancakes are the main food in this area. Flour crushed from sweet potato and corn is used to make the pancake and it tastes just as good as if it were made from wheat flour. Pancakes are also easy to store. People here usually make enough pancakes for five to seven days so that they don't have to cook every day. When they go to work in the mountain, they always take some pancakes wrapped with green onion or something else.

Early the following morning, the wife of my neighbour started to make pancakes. She mixed the flour of sweet potato, corn and soy beans together and made it into a dough. When the pan, which is 60 centimetres in diameter, was hot, she rolled the dough on it and smoothed it out with a bamboo slip. Then a pancake as thin as paper was ready. After she removed it from the pan, she folded it into an oblong shape and served it on the table.

She was very dexterous although she had to tend the kitchen fire while making the pancakes. I was told that before girls got married, they would be asked how well they could make pancakes.

There is no book recording the history of pancakes. Legend has it that during the Warring States Period more than 2,000 years ago, the State of Qin failed to win a battle against the State of Lu because the city wall of Qufu in the State of Lu was too high. When people from the State of Qin heard Lu Ban, a carpenter and brick layer from the State of Lu, had invented the ladder, they asked him to make one for them. When Mo Zi, a philosopher from the State of Lu learned the news, he was very worried and went to the State of Qin to see Lu Ban with a bundle of pancakes. Lu Ban enjoyed the pancakes very much, "It's so delicious! I haven't had them for ages," said Lu Ban.

"But do you want to have them only this one time or more often?" asked Mo Zi.

"Of course I want to have them often," answered Lu Ban.

"But I don't think so," said Mo Zi.

"What do you mean?" Lu Ban was confused.

"The ladder you are making will be used to attack the State of Lu. If our state is conquered, do you think you can still have pancakes?" Suddenly realizing what was going on, he went back to the State of Lu with Mo Zi.

131

132

133

131 Pushing a wheelbarrow to the field or the market, with a passenger balanced among the goods.

132 The villagers build solid houses with rocks collected in the mountains, without using any adhesive.

133 Houses along the coast are roofed with seaweed.

134   Dates, peanuts and apples laid out for guests in a village house.

135   Fried scorpions—a treat for visitors to the Yimeng Mountains.

136   A stone mill lies in the front yard of every household. It is used to grind grain and beans into flour, with which the family make pancakes or steamed bread.

137   Women in rural Shandong Province are regarded as clever or stupid according to their mastery of the indispensable skill of making pancakes.

134

135

136

138   All the village houses in
Weifang—"hometown of New
Year pictures"—are decorated
with New Year pictures, papercuts
and square paintings.

139   "The Unicorn Bestows a
Son," a New Year picture young
couples paste on the door or the
wall of their conjugal room
representing their hope for a son.

138

Weifang New Year Pictures and Zhoucun's Lantern Fair

Besides Yangliuqing in Tianjin and Taohuawu in Suzhou, Weifang in the middle of
Shandong Peninsula is a city known for its New Year woodcuts.

The woodcuts are all printed by hand. The sketch is first drawn by an artist. Then
the printing board is carved according to the sketch. For the coloured woodcuts, an
individual board is carved for each colour. When printing, several boards are fixed on a
table so that one colour is applied on the paper each time. After printing, the boards
are kept for future use.

Weifang New Year pictures are rich in variety. The most common kind is the
horizontal or vertical ones put up on doors and walls, the long pictures above or on
each side of the window, and the ones pasted around a table or a *kang*, a heated brick
bed. The content of the pictures ranges from historical stories and legends to birds,
flowers, fish, insects and symbols expressing good luck.

An even older way of making New Year pictures is still popular in the neighbouring
Gaomi County. Instead of using printing boards, folk artists use a charcoal willow twig
to draw on a piece of paper before patting the charcoal ashes onto the picture, drawing
the lines, applying ink and colour. This kind of pictures is known as ash–patting New
Year pictures. With smooth lines, bold ink splashes and colour application and their free
style of Chinese landscape painting, these drawings are treasured by professional artists.
Unlike woodcutting that can be printed in large quantities, ash–patting can only produce
five or six copies with each sketch.

Gaomi County is also known for its clay toys and papercuts.

Zhoucun, an ancient town not far to the west of Weifang, is a district under the
jurisdiction of Zibo City. It is famous for its annual lantern fair.

139

玉面公主　香王　楊三郎　楊大郎　楊五郎　楊二郎

肖天佑　肖天佑　韓昌　楊八郎　楊七郎　楊六郎　楊四郎

140　This woodcut, taking its theme from the opera "Two Dragons Meet," portrays a patriotic Song Dynasty general Yang Jiye and his exploits in fighting against the invasion of nomads. Woodcuts featuring scenes from popular operas constitute a major genre of New Year pictures in Weifang; they appeal especially to older people.

141　A folk painter in Weifang is printing New Year pictures.

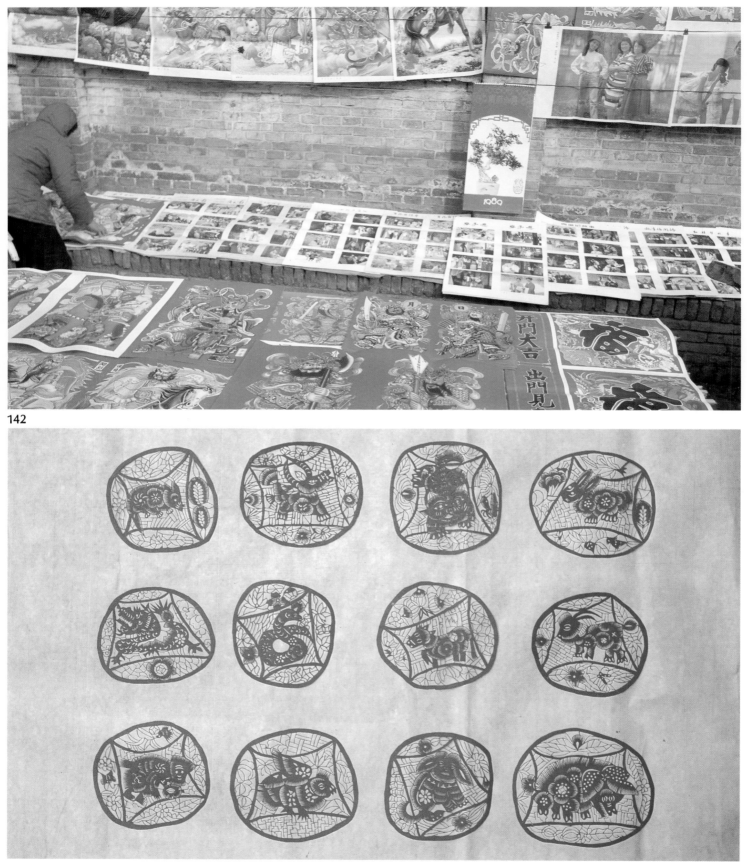

142

143

144

142   New Year pictures of various designs and categories can be found at any local stand.

143   These papercuts from Gaomi depict the twelve animals of the Chinese zodiac: the mouse, ox, tiger, rabbit, dragon, snake, horse, sheep, monkey, chicken, dog and pig. These animals are designated to a year and the animal of the year in which a person is born determines his sign.

144   After farm work, peasants in Gaomi County make clay toys at home. With the children looking on during the process, this creative skill has naturally been passed from one generation to another.

145

As early as in the 17th century, silk reeling and spun silk textile industry had been quite developed. This attracted a lot of merchants to the town and made it prosperous. Every year at around the Lantern Festival on the 15th day of the first lunar month, shops would hang colourful lanterns at the gate and people would light firecrackers and even fireworks to celebrate the holiday. People from nearby villages and merchants came to see the lanterns, do shopping or business. Every night, from the 8th to the 16th of the first month, the town was thronged with people. As the years passed, the lantern fair at Zhoucun became a routine. But there was also exception. It was decided by the Zhoucun residents that the fair would not be held under three circumstances: a poor harvest year, a year of unrest, or a year when there was a natural disaster.

Long before the lantern fair was held, lantern craftsmen would be invited to make lanterns for stores and workshops. People vied with each other in making better and more elegant lanterns. Besides those hung at the gates, lantern towers were also set up at major crossroads.

During the lantern fair, variety shows such as dragon lantern dance, landboat, high stilts, lion dance and *xinzi* are also performed. Of them, *xinzi* is the most unique and traditional show of Zhoucun. Generally a boy or a girl in opera costumes is tied to an iron stick which is tightly fixed onto a socket.

The history of *xinzi* goes back to more than a century. The initiator of this was a local artist. Every year when a show was put up at festival times, he saw that there was such

a large crowd of audiance that people standing behind the crowd could not see what was going on inside the circle. He thought that if the performer could stand at a high place while performing, all in the audiance would be able to see him. Inspired by the candle light, he invented this show on high stick.

At each lantern fair, there were at least a dozen or even a few dozens of *xinzi* shows with the number of performers ranging from ten to several dozens. They would play different roles in local opera.

The heyday of Zhoucun's lantern fair was believed to be during the reign of Emperor Qianlong (1736–1795) of the Qing Dynasty. Although there was no record to prove this, I was a witness to it in 1986 when the fair was held. There were 2,538 lanterns of all kinds, 9 lantern towers at major intersections, 37 *xinzi* shows, 12 dragon lanterns, 42 landboats, 156 pairs of high stilts, 14 pairs of lions dance performers, 95 maskers and 11 floats. There were also some variety shows that I could not name. I suppose even during its heydays, the lantern fair could not have been more spectacular.

131

145   The clay figurines of Gaomi have lively colour patterns.

146   Tiger-head caps for children are believed to have the power to scare off evil spirits.

146

147   During the lantern carnival, the streets in Zhoucun shone with the light from lanterns throughout the night. A shed is set up in the main street, roofed with colourful silk, with lanterns hanging from the roof and along both sides of the street.

148   A popular show unique to Zhoucun, in which actors are fastened to iron props of different heights. In the duet "Honoured Consort Intoxicated," the Honoured Consort appears to be standing on the plate held by the Head Eunuch Gao Lishi.

149   The dance of "big-headed babies."

133

148

149

150   *Collecting Lotus,* a dance by young peasant women.

151   The procession of every village is heralded by the gong–and–drum team, which usually consists of two big drums and a dozen gongs and cymbals.

151

SICHUAN

Chengdu

Jiajiang

Tongliang

Qianwei

VI. The Land of Abundance

SICHUAN Province, situated in southwestern China, is a basin surrounded by high mountain ridges. In ancient times, there were only rugged mountain paths and plank roads built along the face of the cliffs in Sichuan. But today, people can go to Chengdu, the capital of Sichuan, directly from Beijing by train, which is about 2,000 kilometres. When the train approaches the Qinling Mountains, it has to pass through many tunnels. There are 335 tunnels and 998 bridges along the 669-kilometre section of the railway.

In early winter, the Chengdu Plain has a temperate climate and it rains a great deal because the Qinling Mountains keep the cold wind and dust from the north in check. At that time, everything thrives. The fields are crisscrossed with rivers and canals and covered with green wheat sprouts and yellow flowers of the rape plant. Golden-yellow oranges hang from the trees. It was called "the land of abundance" by many generations.

Today, with a population of 100 million, Sichuan Province is one of the main producers of grain, meat, oil-bearing crops, silk, oranges, and medicinal products.

Teahouses

When I was in Chengdu, I saw teahouses everywhere on the streets. There is a saying, "China has the best teahouses in the world and Chengdu has the best teahouses in China." It really has a well-deserved reputation, not only because of the numerous teahouses, but also because the special way of serving and drinking tea.

As soon as the guests enter the teahouse , the waiters or waitresses greet them with a smile on their faces and with teapots and cups in their hands. After the guests have sat down they set the cups on the table and pour the water from behind the guests or from above their heads. When the cups are almost full, the waiters or waitresses raise their hands high suddenly, but not a drop of water is spilled.

The cups which look like antiques have covers and saucers. The cup sitting on the saucer looks like a boat floating on the water, hence the name of "the tea-boat." The cover keeps the water warm and also adjusts the steeping speed of the tea. If you want to drink it immediately after the tea has been made, you can use the cover to strain the tea. So the tea can be soaked well quickly and then it can be drunk. Or the tea can be drunk with the cover on the cup. In this way the tea leaves won't go into the mouth.

People who go to the teahouses are not really thirsty. Retired people pay 20 cents to go to the teahouse and sit there all day long to chat with each other. Sometimes, people bring guests to the teahouses. They eat melon or sunflower seeds while they chat and return home when they are tired of sitting there.

Teahouses are also places for people from various businesses and organizations to get together to hold trade talks or make deals. In recent years, more and more people go to teahouses for business talks. Some of the teahouses also have theatrical performances, such as storytelling, crosstalk (comic dialogue) and Sichuan opera.

In addition, sometimes when people quarrel a mediator will bring them to the teahouse. When their dispute is settled, the person who is in the wrong will pay for the tea. It is interesting that as soon as the quarrellers enter the teahouse and sit down to drink tea, they almost always cool down. With the help of the mediator their disputes can be easily settled. So the teahouses in Sichuan also have special social functions.

152　Enveloped by mountains, Sichuan Province reaches out by way of the Yangtze River, which flows east, cutting across the mountains. This watercourse, consisting of three gorges, is known as the Three Gorges of the Yangtze River. The picture shows a cliff by the river. The plank road on the cliff, constructed in the last century, was used when river traffic was blocked by floods.

153, 154　In the Warring States Period some two thousand years ago, a plank road nearly 800 km in length was built across the Qinling Mountains leading from Shaanxi to Sichuan Province. It sometimes ran across mountain ridges but was for the most part built along the face of cliffs with a path chiseled out of them. The two pictures show relics of the ancient plank road.

152

153　　　　　　　154

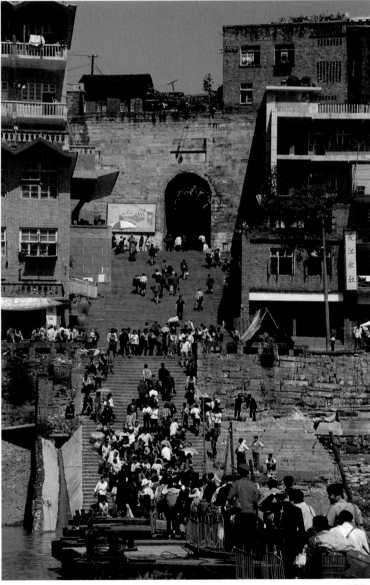

155   The Sichuan–Shaanxi highway built in the 1930's roughly followed the beaten track of the ancient plank road.

156   A village household by the ancient plank road in northern Sichuan.

157   The Yangtze River and its tributaries crisscross all parts of Sichuan, bringing prosperity to the riverside commercial ports. The picture shows Wanxian City, a major port in eastern Sichuan.

158

158   Chess players in a teahouse
in Chengdu.

159   Bird fanciers like to sit in an
outdoor teahouse by the river
bank.

160   A quiet corner for some
private talk.

161   Teapots sit over the stove all
day, with boiling water ready to
make nice cups of tea for
customers.

159

THE LAND OF ABUNDANCE

141

160

161

162

163

The Bamboo World

When you travel in Sichuan you can see bamboo everywhere. The tall bamboos sway gently in the breeze. Buffaloes lie about in the clusters of bamboo.

Sichuan is one of the main bamboo producers in China. At the same time, bamboo is very important in the life of the Sichuan people. There is a saying: "They would rather not eat meat, than live without bamboo." There is a custom that as soon as a new house is built, bamboo trees are planted around the house.

Today people do not wear bamboo shirts, but some people still wear bamboo shoes in some villages or towns. To make the shoes, first they have to smoke the young bamboo to soften it and then use an iron comb to make bamboo hemp. Bamboo shoes are durable, dry and ventilate well. They are also comfortable and grip the ground well, so they are ideal for climbing mountains because they prevent slipping.

Bamboo also can be used as a building material, such as for scaffolds and bridge piers. Bamboo is also used to build dykes. The local people build houses with bamboo. First they weave bamboo slips together and then fix them on a frame. After that mud is applied both on the inside and the outside of the bamboo wall. The beams, which are made of thick bamboo, are strong enough to bear the pressure of the roof made of wheat straw.

There are more than a thousand kinds of household items made of bamboo, such as chairs, tables, tea tables, flower stands, dishes for fruit, pen holders and shelves. When I visited a family, the host showed me a small bamboo basket and said, "On hot summer days if you put several fresh flowers in the basket and hang it outside your mosquito net, you can go to sleep quickly with the fragrant smell of the flowers."

Baskets for firewood and holders for washing rice and vegetables are all made of bamboo and even pot covers are made of bamboo.

164

162   Southern Sichuan features a "sea of bamboo forests."

163   Green bamboo everywhere —surrounding the houses, decorating the parks and lining the roads.

164   It is economical to build bamboo houses in a bamboo forest.

165   One section of the township market is devoted exclusively to bamboo utensils.

Papermaking Workshops

Shiyao Village in Jiajiang County is a famous producer of Chinese traditional paper. Along the stream are beautiful springs and green bamboo all over the mountains. I was told that because of the clear and soft spring water and the fire–fibred bamboo, the paper made there is as soft as cotton and water absorbent, making it the best paper for traditional Chinese painting. About a dozen villages around the stream live from the papermaking industry.

I visited a papermaking workshop there, which was composed of a bamboo–soaking pond, a pot for boiling bamboo, a hammering room and a paper–forming room.

In August of each year, the young bamboo is felled and cut into short pieces which are then pounded. Then the bamboo is put into the lime pond to soak for half a month. After that, the bamboo is taken out and cleaned before being put into the pot to boil. The bamboo should be boiled for a week. Then a group of young men stand around the pot to pound the bamboo with pestles. They sing to the rhythm of the rise and fall of the pestles while they are working. In this way, they do not feel so tired. The fine fibres are washed in bamboo baskets to get rid of the alkaline and then they are stirred by a wood hammer to form a liquid pulp.

Of the 72 steps in papermaking, the most important step is scooping up the pulp. Two people carry a bamboo screen to scoop up the pulp from the jar and then they swing the screen to make the pulp lie flat. After that the liquid is put on the table. When they are solid enough they are put on the wall to dry. Finally, they are cut tidily.

The high–grade paper is white and even. They must be very careful in each step of papermaking, otherwise the quality of the paper will be affected. So in order to guarantee the quality of the paper, the papermaking workshop has its special customs. For example, the workers who pound the bamboo will be served beancurd (*doufu*) to eat because it is thought in this way they will make the paper as white and soft as the beancurd. In addition, words like black and protruding are forbidden in the workshop. These words are considered unlucky. Sometimes when the paper is not white enough or the paper is not even enough, they attribute them to these unlucky words.

I visited Shi's family. On the middle of the living room wall, there was an eye–catching piece of red paper with the words, "Divine seat of our foremaster, Cai Lun." "Do you worship Cai Lun as your God?" I asked. "Yes! If we forget our master we can't make high–quality paper," replied Shi.

Papermaking is one of the four inventions of ancient China. Cai Lun was the creator of papermaking. Before his invention, tortoise shells, bones and metals had been used to write on. Later, bamboo slips and wooden tablets were used. But they were very heavy and inconvenient. With the development of textiles, light and soft silk was used. But the price of silk was too expensive. So when Cai Lun invented a paper made of a pulp composed of hemp, rope ends, rags, and wornout fishing nets, he was immediately praised by the emperor and ministers. From that time on, Cai Lun was considered the founder of papermaking and some people ever considered him as a god.

In Jiajiang, not only a statue and a temple of Cai Lun were built, but a memorial meeting for Cai Lun is held each year in August of the lunar calendar. At that time, pigs and sheep are offered as sacrifices for Cai Lun. For several days, people visit relatives and friends and hold recreational activities.

145

166 The papermaking process recorded in *Exploitation of the Works of Nature*, a Chinese science classic first printed in 1637, has remained basically unchanged to this day in rural paper mills.

167-170   The major procedures
used in rural paper mills:
Wash bamboo chips—the
pulpwood;
Steam the pulpwood into pulp;
Mold paper with a bamboo
screen;
Air the paper in the sun.

168

169

170

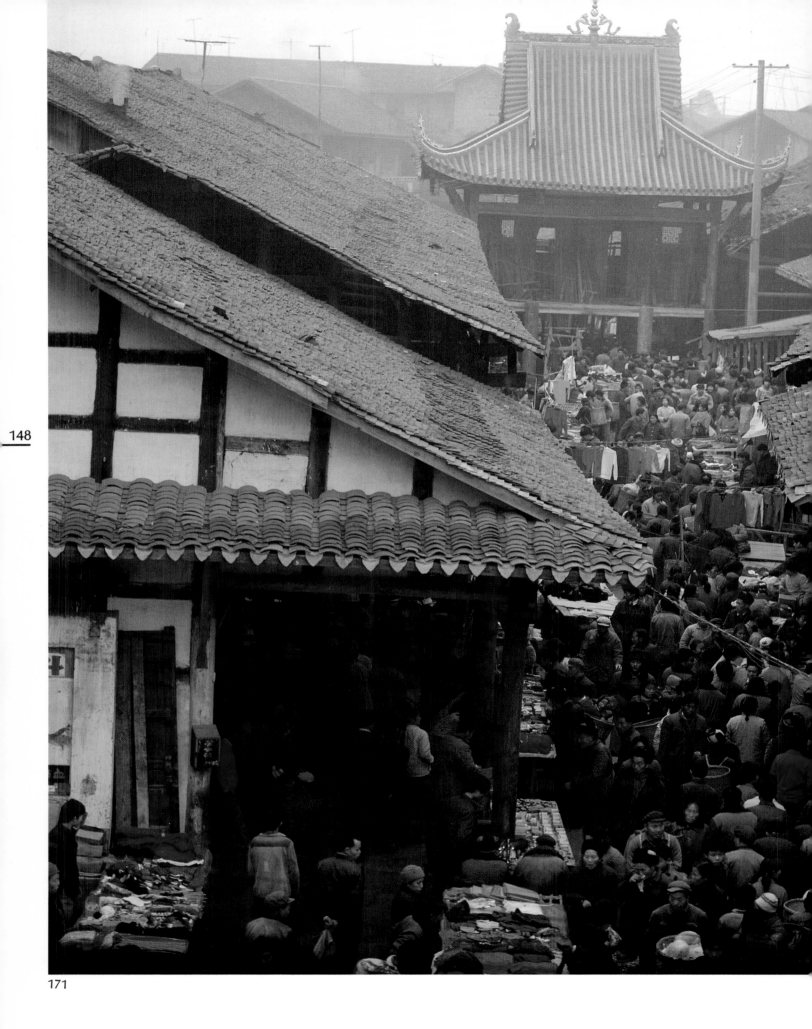

Boat-Shaped Ancient Town

Luocheng Town, built on the top of a mountain in Qianwei County, is peculiarly designed. Different from the straight streets in other towns, the main street in Luocheng is shaped like a boat. Viewed from above, it looks like a boat sailing on a vast green sea.

Luocheng Town was built 300 years ago. People from various places used to come here to do business. This town became an entrepot of goods for and from other places. The boat-shaped design signified the hope that people in the same boat should help each other and live and work in peace and harmony. Another belief is that because the town was built on the top of the mountain water was hard to obtain, so people hoped that the boat-shaped design would bring them water. The second hope became reality when a reservoir was built at the foot of the mountain in 1974. From that time on, it was no longer necessary to transport water there by trucks in the dry season.

On both sides of the street, there are long sheltered market stands four or five metres wide and many shops. At the fair, villagers sell things in the stands where it is cool in summer. The stands also protects people from the sun and rain.

In the middle of the street, an antique gateway and a theatre stand there looking like the forecastle of a freight boat. Here is the centre of the town. When the trade associations or workers and managers of Luocheng Town have conflicts, they use the theatre for their negotiations. At the end of each year, businessmen from various industries get together in the theatre to settle accounts or for business talks. So the theatre functions also as a meeting hall.

At the Lunar New Year and festival times, Sichuan opera is performed in the theatre. On the street, there are other performances, such as *wushu* (martial arts), walking on stilts and imitating the mythical beast unicorn. At these times, the audience will stand or sit on the market stands. People from the nearby villages will turn their baskets upside down to sit on them enjoying the performances.

149

172

171 Luocheng, an ancient boat-shaped town. The building at the crossroads is a theatre.

172 The "stern" of the boat-shaped town.

173   Sichuan has many
ancient towns with diverse local
conditions and customs.
A roadside snack bar selling
rice, bean curd (*midoufu*) and
steamed meat dumplings. Snacks
in Sichuan are varied, delicious and
cheap.

174   Various sorts of cured meat are
on display in a cured meat shop.

173

174

176

177

175

175   Medicinal herbs in short supply in other parts of China, such as the tuber of elevated gastrodia and tendril-leaved fritillary bulb, can be found in any small drugstore in Sichuan.

176   A girl selling flowers by the road. Women in Sichuan like to wear flowers such as michelia, jasmine or cape jasmine in their hair or on their clothing.

177   Village women arrive in town for the fair.

Dragon Dance in the Hometown of the Dragon

Tongliang County can be called the hometown of the dragon. Dinosaur fossils were unearthed from here. The dragon lanterns made in Tongliang County are known far and wide. There is a custom of doing dragon lantern dances during the Lantern Festival (15th of the first lunar month). When it gets dark various dragon dances are done on the streets with colourful lights hanging from above. They look like dragons roaming in a river of light. The dragon with red candle lights in each section is called a fire dragon and the one made of multi-coloured cloth is called a colourful dragon. There is another one called a bench dragon. A one-metre-long bench is divided into three parts, which are connected with iron rings and the dragon head and tail are put on each end. The giant vermes dragon is more than 20 metres long, and is made of 24 sections.

I also saw some children holding up toy straw dragons and Chinese cabbage dragons. The straw dragon is made of rice straw and a bamboo pole. The cabbage dragon is made of a Chinese cabbage with a bamboo pole stuck in it. There is a rope tied to the cabbage and the pole. If it is played at night, a red candle will be stuck on it. The children imitate the movements of the adults, which makes everyone laugh.

Opinions on the origin of the dragon vary. Some people say that the dragon originates from the alligator, pig, or silkworm. Others say that the dragon originates from the worship of lightning and thunder. Still others believe that the dragon is a kind of snake which is respected as a totem of the Huaxia tribe (an ancient name for the Chinese). When the Huaxias annexed other clans, the other clan symbols, such as deer, camels, fish, tigers and eagles were combined to create the dragon of today.

There are many legends about dragons. In the Han Dynasty, people thought dragons could summon clouds and rain. So when there was arid weather, they would do the dragon dance to seek help from the dragon. This custom has passed from generation to generation and exists even today.

The legends about the dragon dance in Tongliang goes that one day when the Dragon King of the East Sea got a serious backache, he disguised himself as an old man so he could see a doctor on the land. After feeling his pulse, the doctor asked in surprise, "Are you a human being?" The Dragon King had to tell the truth. So the doctor asked him to turn back to his original form and took out a centipede from a scale in his waist and drew out pus by applying a plaster to the affected part. He was cured. In order to show his gratitude the Dragon King revealed his secret. He told the doctor, "You'll have good weather for the crops this year if you make dragons like me and play with them."

I was surprised to see that when the dragon dance was at its peak, they threw firecrackers and fireworks at the dragon lanterns. So the activity ended in an atmosphere of excitement.

Why did they burn the dragon lantern? One belief is that when the dragons are burned they go to heaven which makes the weather good for the crops. Another belief is that when the dragons are burned they repel all bad luck and disasters.

Sometimes the young men who play the dragon lanterns will catch the fancy of girls. Those young men are considered lucky young men.

178   The people of Tongliang are skilled at making dragon lanterns. The picture shows a dragon lantern with a head of paper and a trunk of coloured cloth.

178

179

180

181

182

179   Several dragons are used in the performance of the dragon dance.

180   Spurting fire, the dragon boat rides on the river at night.

181   People living by the river used to send forth floating lanterns as a sacrifice for the drowned. The ancient custom has become a festival activity today.

182   This girl is releasing a lotus lantern, along with a secret wish, into the stream.

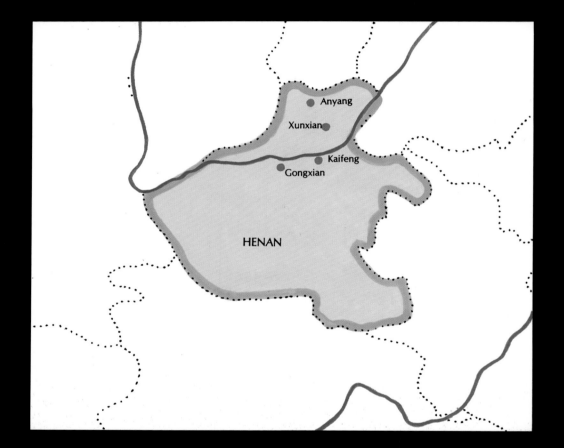

VII. Customs of the Central Plains

LOCATED in the central part of China, in the middle and lower Yellow River valley, Henan Province was called the Central Plains in ancient times and is one of the cradles of the Chinese nation. The ruins in the suburbs of the city of Anyang were at one time the capital of the Shang Dynasty (16th–11th centuries B.C.). The inscriptions on bones and bronze vessels unearthed here show the splendid culture of 3,000 years ago. My trip to collect folk stories in Henan Province started from Anyang.

Village Fair

When I arrived in Xunxian County south of Anyang, the Tiancang Festival Fair was being held in Niucun Village. I had never seen such a grand and lively spectacle before.

The Tiancang (Heavenly Barn) Festival on the 20th of the fist lunar month is also called "Filling the Barn Festival." After eating millet gruel in the courtyard, farmers sprinkle circles of pan ashes symbolizing barns or set up "storehouses" with sorghum stalks. They fill the barns and storehouses with cereals which is a symbol for their hope for an abundant harvest.

Legend has it that the Tiancang Festival dates back to the times of remote antiquity. One day, two clans, the Gong Gong and the Zhuan Xu, were fighting against each other. After Gong Gong, the head of the clan, was defeated he hit the high Buzhou Mountain angrily, which touched off a downpour and floods. Fortunately, the deity, Nu Wa, mended the sky with the magical Five Colour Stones. The flood stopped and people were once more safe and sound. It is said that the day of mending the sky was on the 20th day of the first lunar month, so it is also called "Mending the Sky Day."

In the past, Niucun and nine other villages often held the Tiancang Festival Fair in turn since they frequently suffered from floods. They first offered sacrifices to the Temple of the Dragon King, praying that the Dragon King could stop floods. Every household, in the meantime, hung cakes on the central room of their house, kitchen and eaves for Nu Wa to use when she mended the sky.

At noon, teams of bands, flags and salvo from the ten villages arrived. The performers of *wushu* (martial arts), lion dance, stilts, landboats and running donkeys were ready to perform. A big box with seats in it, carried like a sedan chair, was almost ready. It was three or four metres high. In the procession, eight strong men would carry the box in which two girls dressed in the style of traditional opera characters sat. A villager in his fifties from Niucun Village—the organizer of the fair, waved an apricot yellow flag, a salute was fired and the bands began playing music. The entertainment teams from different villages started out in an orderly procession.

There were performances at the entrance to the village and on the streets, with colourful flags. Crowds of people stood everywhere, some even on the roofs of houses and on the tops of walls.

Wushu performers gave performances with spears, staffs, swords, and knives. After the double lions dance, a strong man began fighting with a person dressed up as a lion. Finally the "lion" was defeated and withdrew from the competition. Two young men wearing masks which made them look like children, imitated naive children making the audience laugh as did a boatman paddling a landboat, when he sang a humorous song accompanied by movements.

Although night fell, the performance still went on. The lions were dancing in throngs and sacrifices were offered to the God of Fire who was said to have the power to dispel fire disasters. Firecrackers over 50 metres long, which hung on trees, began crackling and spluttering, which went on for more than forty minutes. The Tiancang Festival Fair, which was prosperous for the whole day, ended with the sound of firecrackers symbolizing good harvest, happiness, safety and peace.

183   During the Tiancang Festival, which used to be an occasion for offering sacrifices to the gods, farmers stop working for a day and swarm to the village square to watch performances.

184   Though few people today still believe in the Dragon King as the controller of all rivers and lakes, the sacrificial ceremony to the Dragon King has remained popular. It is one of the highlights of the Tiancang Festival.

184

185

186

187

185   Young girls, dressed in
colourful costumes, ride from
village to village to give
performances.

186   The festival would be
incomplete without a show of
Henan opera.

187   Elderly women are the most
enthusiastic audience of Henan
opera.

188

188   On the Tiancang Festival some villagers, mostly elderly women, go to the temple to worship the gods.

189   In the temple, some village
women offer hanging screens they
have embroidered to the gods and
ask for their blessing.

189

Town of Toys

Junxian County is widely renowned for its folk toys. While at the fair, I saw vendors' stands piled high with all kinds of toys—wooden knives, spears, swords and halberds, tigers and rabbits made of cloth, wood carving, small lovely horses, lions with moving heads and roosters and birds which could make sounds.

When chatting with several vendors of clay toys, I found out that they were all from Yangqi Village. Legend has it that Yang Qin was a leader of a rural insurrectionary army, 1,300 years ago. He led a campaign, for three days and nights, capturing a grain depot here, which he used to store grain and station troops. When burying the bodies of their fallen companions, soldiers thought that pottery figurines and daily necessities should be buried with the dead soldiers, so that they might use them in the other world. However, where could they obtain the things to bury with the dead soldiers? Craftsmen in the insurrectionary army who could work with clay, found that the clay on the banks of the river had good viscosity and didn't crack after being heated. So they dug clay and sculpted clay figures and clay horses to be buried with the dead. Since then, Yangqi Village has had a tradition of making clay toys.

When the time of the fair was approaching, everyone in the village — men and women, old and young comprising more than 700 households, were busy day and night. They dug yellow clay and dried it in the sun, pulverized and sifted it. They mixed the clay with water and added cotton or paper pulp to it. Finally they rubbed and hammered the mixture with a wooden rod till it became soft and could be kneaded.

I saw a 70-year-old craftsman named Wang Tingliang sculpt clay toys that day. He finished sculpting a buffalo in two minutes and a lion in three minutes. The bold lines reflected the movements of the animals. After the clay toys were dried, they were baked on a kitchen range for a while and then a coat of rosin is applied. Finally, patterns and designs were drawn on the toys in red, green or white. Baskets of clay toys were made and sold at the fairs.

163

190   A roadside stand selling clay figurines. Many of the peddlers' ancestors had served in the ranks of an insurgent peasant army.

190

191   The old couple are making clay figurines. Every household in Yangqi Village is virtually a small clay sculpture mill.

192   Painting the clay figurines demands some knowledge of painting. Works of painting and calligraphy are therefore a major drawing-room asset for most households in Yangqi Village.

191

192

193 A village by the Yellow
River. At the back of the village in
the distance, the shelter–forest
stands on the embankment of the
river.

193

Taking Precautions Against the Waters of the Yellow River

The Yellow River, renowned for its yellow turbid water, is the second largest river in China and has also been the scene of many disasters. When the rainy season comes each year, the rainwater carries silt and sand from the Loess Plateau into the Yellow River. A ballad goes: "One *shi* of the Yellow River water can settle six *dou* of sand (*shi*

and *dou* are Chinese measurements of weight, 1 *shi* = 60 kilogrammes, 1 *dou* = 6 kilogrammes). When the Yellow River enters its middle and lower reaches, its speed slows down because the riverbed is wider there. Out of 1.6 billion, 0.4 billion tons of silt carried by the river are deposited and the rest flows into the ocean. Therefore, the more silt that accumulates, the higher the riverbed becomes, and the higher dykes should be built. If a flood comes or the river dyke is not in good condition, the river will overflow its banks. Over 1,500 overflows of the river dykes have been recorded in the past 2,000 years and the river has changed its course 26 times. The floods brought enormous disasters to the people living on the banks of the Yellow River. In order to combat the disastrous floods, the villages located along the Yellow River have many unique customs.

Outan is a small village, located in a suburb of Kaifeng, an ancient capital. Rural buildings covered by the shade of trees are built on one- or two-metre-high earth platforms, called house platforms by the villagers. Outan Village is situated in the river flat, one metre lower than the river north of the village. When a heavy downpour comes, the flood will overflow the river's banks and inundate the village. So, no one knows from what time villagers began building house platforms to guard against disastrous floods. The trees in front of and behind the houses are not only shelters from rain but can also stop the materials carried by the flood from dashing against the houses and washing them away.

The Yellow River has four annual flood seasons. When the flood season approaches, the villages sends people to inspect the dykes of the river. When the flood peak is coming, the elderly, children and food are sent to relatives in villages located on higher elevations. For this reason, parents in Outan Village all wish to marry their children to people living in those villages, so that they will have shelters when the flood comes. Women make steamed cakes and pack the luggage. Men hang wooden plates on tree branches in case of a flood. They also hang chains of dried radish slices and dried sweet potato slices on tree branches and the eaves of houses for those who climb trees and to the eaves to avoid floods, but they can also be eaten when people return to the village. The custom in the region is that anyone can eat the dried sweet potato slices hanging on tree branches and eaves, without being condemned.

When the flood is coming, gongs are sounded in the village. Hearing the sound of the gongs, every household takes down the door plank to make a raft. They carry their clothes wrapped in cloth, food, and pots, bowls, ladles and basins to flee from the flood by raft. Because of frequent floods, villagers don't have the habit of buying furniture. When people leave their doors open, nothing will be lost.

The local farmers' houses are simple thatched cottages. The cottages are made of adobe except the four corners, which are made of brick columns. When steeped in the flood, the adobe wall will collapse. As long as the four brick columns remain standing, the roof will still remain. After fleeing from the flood, people will rebuild the adobe wall. Hence, it is called the "water passing house"—the adobe wall may fall down but the roof may not collapse when the floods hit the house.

In the last 30 to 40 years, because dykes have been built, disastrous floods have decreased. Farmers begin building houses with bricks and tiles instead of using adobe. However, when people built homes, they will, according to tradition, first build a house platform rather than dig down to build a foundation.

In the autumn harvest season, the threshing ground is a busy place. To cultivate the land, one must know the characteristics of the Yellow River. In winter and spring, high and stable yields of winter wheat are expected because of low water. In summer and

167

194

autumn the dangers of flood are frequent and the yield of autumn crops is uncertain. However, the planting of such high-stemmed crops as sorghum and corn is very useful because they can ease the turbulent flood when it comes. When a small flood comes, the silt left over from the flood is good fertilizer for high-stemmed crops. Besides, the sorghum stalks are indispensable for protecting dykes and for emergencies.

A lot of boat-like shallow baskets are put in the threshing ground. Women thresh sesame and peel the corn. Waterproof, shallow wicker baskets are used for holding food. Once the flood hits the village, children can be put into the wicker baskets which become small life emergency boats.

Like the foundation of a house, the threshing ground is very large and high. Ordinarily, it is used for threshing crops. When the flood comes, villagers carry wooden beds, food and other necessities to leave on the threshing ground, so they call the threshing ground the "water avoiding platform."

With an area of 2,600 square metres and three metres high, the threshing ground is not big enough to hold the 240 villagers in Outan Village. So the village is planning to enlarge the platform to set up a new village on the platform.

195

194   Villagers often build a shrine beside the gate, hoping thereby to secure peace and safety for the family.

195   The corn to be used as seeds are hung around the courtyard not only to dry them, but also to signify a good harvest.

196   These two older women, who live in a remote village, belong to the last generation of Chinese women who have suffered the inhuman practice of foot binding.

197   Village women make pretty cloth toys.

169

196

198   A bicycle ride for the whole family along a country road.

199   In rural Henan, it is customary for people to eat their meals in the courtyard while chatting with neighbours.

198

199

Skylight Cave Dwellings

East Village in Gongxian County looks like a loess hill from afar. No houses can be seen. So when a tour guide said there were 1,200 families there, I was perplexed as to where the villagers lived.

Upon entering the village, I found a unique world of cave dwellings. The cave dwellings are different from those of northern Shaanxi Province which were dug beside mountains. The cave dwelling is a square hole dug underground and since the cave dwelling is similar to a skylight, it is called a skylight cave dwelling. Some cave dwellings are durable and solid for a thousand years because they are made of solid earth. Nanyaowan in Gongxian County is the hometown of Du Fu (712–770), a famous poet in the Tang Dynasty. The cave dwelling, in which Du Fu was born, has remained intact.

A skylight cave dwelling in which the families of two brothers live together, is 12 metres long and wide and 8 metres high. On the four sides are three arched doors. Besides the door towards the ground in the southeast, there are 11 rooms.

The host invited us to visit his room. The room was three metres wide and seven metres long, and desks, chairs and cupboards were arranged on one side of the room. "Where are the beds?" Hearing this, the host drew back the curtain to reveal a niche with the beds in it. Small niches are dug into the wall to store food, dishes, condiments, pots and cooking utensils among other household goods. All these niches make the cave dwellings tidy and comfortable.

The advantages of cave dwelling are that they are heat–insulated, cool in summer and warm in winter. The disadvantages are that cave dwellings have poor lighting and ventilation and they are damp in summer. After leaving the cave, one has to climb hills, which is difficult for the elderly who have trouble moving about. What is more, the cave dwellings can't bear continuous downpours. Low walls are built around the cave dwellings to prevent rainwater from flowing into the caves, and seepage pits are dug to contain water, so it can seep into the ground. If it rains hard and the seepage pits are full of water, the water will overflow into the caves and the caves could collapse.

In the past, farmers were very poor. They thought that building earth houses was cheaper than building houses with brick, tile and wood. Now that the farmers are better–off, they have calculated that it takes too much time and effort to dig cave dwellings and it occupies too much land to build them. In recent years, there has been a great upsurge in the construction of brick houses. Two newly established brick factories in the village have more demands than they can meet.

Perhaps farmers are sentimentally attached to the cave dwellings which were handed down from generation to generation, so when they build brick houses on flat ground, they still build houses with arch–shaped doors in the style of a cave dwelling.

173

200   People who live in skylight cave–dwellings have to climb dozens of steps to reach the ground.

200

201   The courtyard in a skylight cave–dwelling.

202   The ground serves as the roof for these cave–dwellings.

203   Oil–lamps are used in many cave–dwellings. By custom, a red paper is pasted beside the lamp with the warning, "Be careful of lamp fire."

204   The flat roof is a good place for drying grain in the sun.

202

203

204

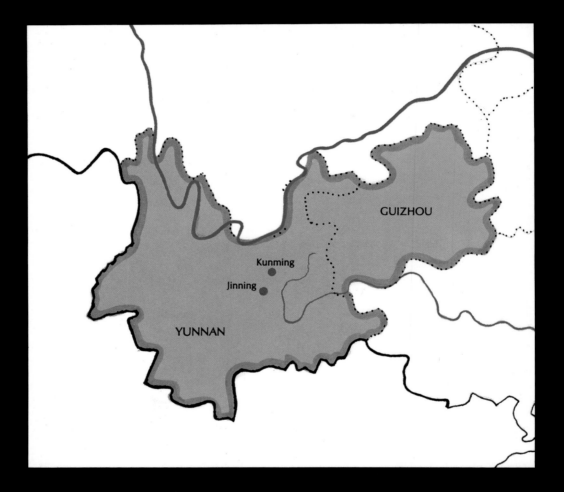

VIII. Local Customs in a Border Area

YUNNAN Province on the southwest border is the home of 23 minority nationalities besides the Hans, including the Yi, Dai, Bai, Tibetan, Naxi, Miao and Jingpo nationalities. Neighbouring Guizhou Province on the Yunnan–Guizhou Plateau is also inhabited by many different ethnic groups. The harmonious coexistence of different minority groups over the past centuries has contributed a great deal to the acceptance of each other's customs. In spite of the differences that remain, they share a lot in common.

"Magpie Dress"

In the Yunnan local dialect, a small intermontane plain is called a *bazi*. Baofengba in Puning County is a village inhabited by the Hans. When I saw Luo Meiying, the township leader, she wore a typical peasant dress: a black cloth scarf wrapped on her head, a white tight jacket covered with a black lace vest, an embroidered apron around her waist, blue pants and embroidered cotton shoes. Sensing my curiosity, she told me that it was called a magpie dress because the black scarf and vest and white sleeves made her look like a magpie with its black head and body and white wings.

The magpie dress was introduced to this Han village by Luo Meiying from her Yi village when she got married more than 12 years ago. She then changed the chintz scarf and white vest to black, making her look like a magpie which is regarded by the Chinese as a lucky bird. They believe that if a magpie sings in the tree in front of your house, your family will be fortunate.

Yi girls are known for their simplicity, beauty and kindness. Young men from Baofengba think themselves very lucky if they can marry Yi girls. They get to know each other while cutting firewood in the mountains, at country fairs and singing, dancing or drinking mountain wine at local festivals or activities.

When I visited a Yi village called Tianba, I saw a *tiyue* (dancing) scene. According to the Yi custom, Yi girls can only dance with young men from other villages instead of those from their own village. For the occasion, young men from Han villages bring wine, sausages and candies to the appointed place and start a fire while waiting. When the Yi girls arrive, they all get up and greet them before sitting down around the fire and chatting over the picnic. Then, they stand up and dance around the fire, while the Yi girl ties an embroidered purse on the waist of the man she likes.

But if a young man breaks his promise by not showing up at the appointed place, the Yi girl gathers some brambles and puts them on the designated meeting spot to show her disappointment, thus breaking up the relationship.

At Tianba, the old Yi houses with thick walls made of sticky soil look as solid as a castle. In the past, there was always a dog crouching on the flat roof to watch out for people who came to attack the village. The frequent contact over the past few decades

205

206

205 Terraced fields in the Ailao Mountain area in Yunnan Province. Since ancient times, people in the mountainous areas of Yunnan and Guizhou have cultivated terraced fields suited to the shape of the mountain and the quality of the soil.

206 The Yunnan-Guizhou Plateau has abundant forest resources. Lumberers bind logs into rafts and let them drift down the river to the collecting posts.

207 Old-fashioned water wheels are still in use in Guizhou, where the cultivated land often lies above water level.

207

between the Yi and the Han has also resulted in intermarriage between the Yi and the Han. When the Yis found that the Han's brick houses with slanted roofs were durable and good for drainage, they also started to build their houses as the Hans do.

I was invited by a Yi family of Guo Xiaolan. They lived in a two-storey house. Entering the arched gateway, I found myself in a small yard with a sitting room and bedroom in front and two rooms on each side: one that served as a kitchen and the other that served as a storehouse. It looked quite similar to the houses found in the Han village of Baofengba.

It was the slack winter season. A few young people from the Tianba amateur singing and dancing troupe were practising the Flower Lantern Opera, a folk opera which used to be popular among the Hans in Yunnan and Guizhou. During the Spring and Lantern festivals, a group of three to five performers would bring simple costumes with them and give performances from village to village.

After generations of intermingling with the minorities, the Han people have also been influenced by them in clothing and customs.

The Miao women are good at dyeing, weaving and embroidery. Not only do they wear colourful embroidered dresses, but they also dress their children in colourful clothes. Even the bundle cloth they use to carry baby on the back is also embroidered with beautiful patterns. Imitating the Miao women, the Han women also make embroidered hats for their children and carry their babies with embroidered bundle cloths on their backs. It is difficult to tell a Miao woman from a Han from their back. Assimilating and developing the best of different minorities, some Han women in minority-inhabited areas dress themselves in colourful minority costumes, and yet no one can identify them with any particular minority group.

The Han women living at Baofengba of Jinning all wear embroidered cotton shoes. As the shoe has an upturned tip which looks like a turtledove's head, it is known as turtledove shoe. Though most of the minority women living in Yunnan and Guizhou provinces also wear embroidered shoes, no one can say for sure who the originator is.

208   A folk saying in Guizhou goes, "the ground never remains level for more than a metre." This topography has resulted in a unique style of architecture. In the undulating and confining terrain, houses are supported by wooden pillars on the one side and lean against the mountain slope on the other.

209   In central Yunnan Province, the construction of houses begins with the wall, which is made of rammed clay, upon which wooden pillars and beams and tiles are subsequently added.

210   The Miao women in Guizhou are good at weaving, dyeing and embroidery. They use homemade cloth and embroidery to dress and decorate themselves and their children.

208

209

211   The Han women in Yunnan and Guizhou provinces are also in the habit of strapping their babies on their backs. They rival the Miao women in their embroidery skills.

212   The "turtledove shoes," popular among the Han women in Jinning.

212

213

Funeral Customs

On my return to Baofengba, I learned that many villagers had gone to Housuo Village to attend the funeral of an elderly woman named Yin Caiyun. I decided to go and started off at night.

The main room served as the mourning hall. Red candles were placed in front of the casket which was flanked by pine branches and red and green paper balls and flowers. After relatives and friends bowed to the deceased, lit the incense and candles, they presented the family with glutinous rice cakes, candies and wine. Then they took turns standing by the casket. When the family started to cry for the loss of a family member, eight men and women with drums on their waists, led by a man with a wooden dragon head in his hand, started to dance to the beat of the drums in vigorous steps. When the music stopped, the dancers started to walk slowly, singing a mourning song.

According to the Han custom, a mourning ceremony includes paying respects to the deceased, gift-giving and a banquet given by the family of the deceased to express their thanks to friends and relatives. Villagers from Baofengba adopted the Yi's way of mourning because they thought getting the whole village together to dance and sing at the ceremony was a good way to show their respect for the dead and consolation to the family.

213   Influenced by the customs of the Yi nationality, the Han people in Baofengba also include the drum dance in funeral processions.

214   At the funeral, the coffin is carried over a line of family members of the dead person who are prostrated on the ground.

214

215

215 The villagers perform the drum dance to herald the bier.

216 For every hundred metres on the way, the funereal contingent stops to walk around the coffin, singing and dancing.

216

217 When the coffin is lowered into the pit, it will not be buried until the family members of the dead have scattered some earth over it.

217

When I left the village I could still hear the loud mourning song:

It is very hard to find a thousand–year–old tree in the mountain,
It is also not easy to find a hundred–year–old person in the world.

I was told that the guests attending the mourning ceremony would take turns to sing and dance all through the night. When the funeral procession was held on the following morning, the family members of the deceased would walk in front, holding the mourning streamer. The younger generation in the family were required to kneel down, letting the casket pass overhead. On the way, people would stop after walking every hundred metres to sing and dance around the casket until it was buried in the mountain.

On the third day after I came back to Baofengba from Housuo Village, I attended a wedding of a Han family. On the wedding day, when the dressed–up groom came to the bride's house, he was grandly welcomed. A dinner had been prepared especially for him. The most eye–catching of the dishes was a steamed whole chicken with a yellow flower in its beak.

After finishing dinner, the groom was ready to take the bride to his home. The bridegroom walked in front, followed by the bride who was carried by her brother. The Han custom requires that when the bride leaves home, her feet should not touch the ground. But I never expected to see this practice in such a remote and small village in Yunnan Province.

The bride was dressed in a red jacket and blue pants. Instead of covering her face with a red scarf, she held a black cotton umbrella to hide her face. Hanging on her chest was a mirror which was believed to be able to drive away evil spirits.

218 Having come to fetch his bride, the bridegroom is feted with a table of wine and dishes all to himself.

219 The dowry must contain shoes of both patterned and single-colour cloth handmade by the bride herself. These will serve as presents to the bridegroom's parents and relatives.

220 The bride is carried away from the home of her parents.

218

219

221   The bride wears a mirror
around her neck and holds an
umbrella to conceal her face.

221

Exorcising Ghosts Opera

I had heard a long time ago that Guizhou was the only place where an ancient opera of primitive culture, the exorcising ghosts opera (*nuoxi*), was still played. On my trip to Guizhou this time, I happened to see a few shows.

The performers were all farmers. The accompanying musical instruments included gongs, drums, and cymbals. With simple costumes and masks, they danced to the improvised beat. Whenever there was a show, people would stream there to enjoy the performance. Although this opera died out long ago in its birthplace, it still lives on in a border province hundreds of miles away.

The exorcising ghosts opera originated from a sacrificial ceremony for driving away evil and pestilence in ancient times. The unearthed objects from the Yin ruins in Henan Province showed the mask worn by the official of the exorcising ceremony. It proves that this kind of ceremony was practised in court as far back as 3,000 years ago. The earliest record of this ceremony was found in the *Rites of Zhou*, a book recording the system of the court of the Zhou Dynasty (c. 11th century–221 B.C.). It reads, "With eyes shining like gold, bear paws over his palms and a red coat over his shoulders, a masked man waved a spear and a shield and led a hundred slaves to exorcise the pestilence...."

By the Han (206 B.C.–A.D. 220) and Tang (618–907) dynasties, the scale of the court exorcising ceremony grew even larger. "Masked Dance" and "Dance of Twelve Gods" appeared in the Han Dynasty. Folk exorcising dances became popular and more entertaining, with stories added to the rituals of offering sacrifices to the gods and exorcising ghosts.

During the Song Dynasty (960–1279), the plot of the story became more complicated and complete, and its masks more varied. Gradually, the ceremony developed into an opera.

By the 13th to 14th centuries, *zaju*, poetic dramas set to music, flourished in the Yuan Dynasty (1271–1368). Instead of wearing masks, performers painted their faces with colourful paint and the exorcising opera was also replaced by different local operas. By the Song Dynasty (960–1279), the exorcising ghosts opera was introduced to China's southwest area by war refugees from the Central Plains. Later in the Ming Dynasty (1368–1644), soldiers stationed in the Guizhou border area also brought the opera there from the interior.

Now, the exorcising opera and many of its offshoots are still popular in Guizhou.

However, the exorcising opera and sacrificial rite dance popular among the ethnic groups such as the Yi and Bouyei still remain at their early stage, similar to the sacrificial rites practised in the Zhou Dynasty. With its complicated plot, the exorcising opera in northeast Guizhou has reached the zenith of its development.

This opera is characterized by various masks made by local artists. In Guizhou, there are almost a thousand exorcising opera troupes and each one has some masks handed down from previous generations.

Looking at the masks, I could not but admire the ingenuity of those who carved them. By the hands of a skilled artisan, a piece of lifeless wood was transformed into an image full of artistic power. Ghost or human, every one of them looks unique and vivid. Further-more, the performers' exaggerated gestures and humorous lines also add dramatic effect to the masks. Though already different from their original form, these bold and vivid masks still capture attention with their artistic beauty.

191

222

223

222 A courtyard, a spacious
central room or a village lot can be
the site for the performance of
nuoxi, a style of folk opera that has
evolved from a ritual dance for
dispelling ghosts. All the female
roles are played by men.

223 Wearing a mask, the actor
enjoys the status of a god for the
moment and can relish the fruits,
wine and provisions proffered by
the villagers.

224

224 The masks in the *nuoxi*, with
their simplistic design and
inscrutable expressions, are a
combination of art and religion.

225, 226　The colourful masks used in the exorcising opera.

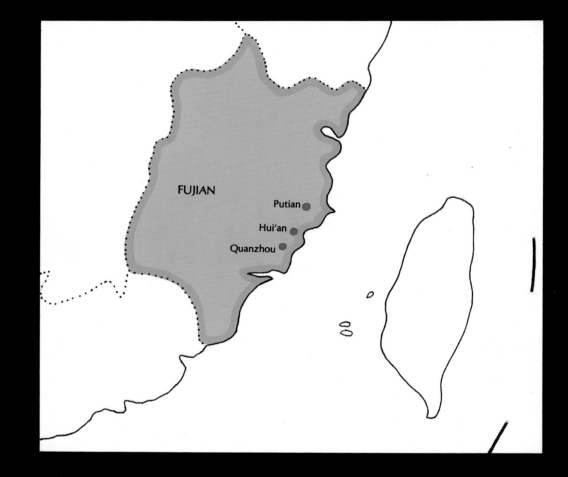

IX. Customs of Quanzhou and Hui'an in Fujian Province

FUJIAN Province is situated on the southeastern coast of China. It has a warm, humid sub–tropical climate, so plants are green all year. In early spring, when it is still cold in Beijing, Fujian already enjoys a sunlit and enchanting spring. All kinds of flowers are in bloom. Litchi, longan and loquat trees blossom into yellow flowers. The ancient green banyans with their clusters of gnarled roots are like old men with long beards.

Lantern Festival

When we arrived at Quanzhou, it was the 15th day of the first lunar month—*Yuanxiao Jie*, known as the Lantern Festival. Each year, there is an exhibition of coloured lanterns at night. Every family hangs red lanterns over their gates. Children carry all kinds of coloured lanterns and in streets and squares, coloured lantern sheds are built for lantern exhibition. Everyone goes out to see the lanterns.

The Lantern Festival is a traditional festival in China. The way of making the lanterns differs according to the natural environment. Lanterns are different in the north and the south. In Northern Shaanxi Province, women in the countryside use sorghum stalks to make lantern frames, then they paste red paper on the frames. In this way, they make all sorts of lanterns, such as pumpkin lanterns, persimmon lanterns and sheep lanterns. They also cut potatoes into a bowl shape. Then they put oil into the bowl–shaped potatoes and place lampwicks in them and cover the potatoes with red paper lampshades. People hang red lanterns over the gates of their cave dwellings. Willow trees are also decorated with coloured paper. Red lanterns are hung here and there on willow trees. The trees are called lantern trees or spark trees.

Beijing was the capital of several dynasties in Chinese history. On the Lantern Festival, all sorts of lanterns were hung in the palace. Artists made fancy lanterns, whose frames were made with carved fine wood. They covered lanterns with silk, gauze, glass and sliced ox horn on which pictures of landscapes, flowers and birds were painted. At that time, lantern exhibitions in Beijing had already become large and colourful. Present–day Dengshikou (Lantern Fair Gateway) near Wangfujing Street was where lantern exhibitions were held at that time.

Harbin in North China is called an ice city. All sorts of lanterns are made there with ice. The sparking, crystal–clear lanterns are really beautiful.

Fujian has an abundance of rain, so the buildings on both sides of its streets all have overhanging upper storeys known as *qi lou* to shelter pedestrians from the rain. On the Lantern Festival colourful lanterns are hung over the *qi lou*. Streets sometimes have thousands of coloured lanterns hung along them.

Lanterns come in different shapes, such as bird, animal, flower and fish. Some lanterns are shaped like fruit, such as oranges, litchis, pineapples and others. Some are very modern like rocket and satellite lanterns. Fragrant smells waft in the breeze from the lanterns. Sandalwood incense is burned in octagonal palace lanterns.

Quanzhou has unique local customs. On the second day of the first lunar month, newly-married couples bring New Year's gifts to the woman's parents. When the couple returns home, the parents give them two lotus lanterns, one white and the other red. On the night of the Lantern Festival, the young couple hang them beside their bed, and then they light candles in the two lanterns. After that they wait and see which candle burns out first. If the candle in the white one burns out first, it means they will have a baby boy; if the candle in the red one burns out first, it means they will have a girl.

In previous times, young women and men did not have free social contact. Therefore, the Lantern Festival became an opportunity to look for marriage partners. There is a famous love story from ancient times among the people of Quanzhou. At the Lantern Festival, a young man named Chen San met a young woman from a rich family named Huang Wuniang. They fell in love at first sight. But Wuniang's father was greedy for money and power. He betrothed his daughter to Lin Da from a rich family. So Chen San disguised himself as a tradesman who polished bronze mirrors. He went to Huang's home to polish their bronze mirror and broke the bronze mirror purposely. To pay for the mirror, he sold himself into the Huang family as a slave. By doing so, he had the chance to meet Wuniang secretly. At last he and Wuniang ran away from the family and got married.

198

227   A village in southern Fujian Province. The soil and climate in Fujian are favourable for the growth of banyan trees. Ancient banyan trees with big canopies and sprawling roots can be found everywhere in both urban and rural areas. The provincial seat, Fuzhou, is known as the "city of banyan trees."

227

228

228 The city of Quanzhou in southern Fujian is shaped like a carp. The main street, five kilometres in length, runs across the city. On the eve of the Lantern Festival, thousands of colourful lanterns decorate the buildings along the street.

229 With the approach of the Lantern Festival, the streets are lined with lantern vendors.

230 The lanterns which the children are holding are probably presents from their grandmothers. It is customary in Quanzhou for grandmothers to buy lanterns for their grandchildren for the Lantern Festival.

199

229

230

231

231   Fishermen have a preference for fish-shaped lanterns as a token of luck for a bumper catch.

232   During the Lantern Festival, the street is packed with people watching the dragon-dance performance.

233   The Chest Patting Dance.

234   The light, comical Fire Tripod Dance signifies prosperity and happiness.

232

Local Dances

On the night of the Lantern Festival, colourfully-decorated lanterns were lit, so Quanzhou became a sea of lanterns. Old and young people alike went out to streets, parks and stadiums in high spirits to see the lanterns. At the same time, they had the chance to see performances. Theatrical troupes from schools, factories, institutions, stores and rural areas came to the city centre square to give performances. The dance named Chest Patting Dance is quite interesting. Several dancers with bare feet wear straw hoops on their heads and they are stripped to the waist. With vigorous movements they pat their shoulders, chests, arms and thighs with their hands. Accompanied by a drum, the dancers also sing while they dance. Though this kind of dance is very simple, its bold and unconstrained movements are both invigorating and graceful.

The Chest Patting Dance was probably a local dance in ancient times. During harvest time, farmers with bare chests usually took a short break when they were cutting rice. They did not have musical instruments and costumes, so they wrapped straw ropes round their heads and inserted rice ears on the ropes as decoration. They clapped their hands and patted their chests in order to express their happiness for a good harvest. At the same time, this dance relaxed their muscles and gave them a break. Gradually, these gestures developed into the Chest Patting Dance. The next performance was the Fire Tripod Dance. It shows a wedding ceremony from the past. The shy bride and bridegroom accompanied by attendants came to the stage. Carrying a fire tripod with a roaring fire in it, the groom's parents walked in front, singing and dancing. Holding an earthen ware bowl with salt and wheat bran in it, the matchmaker threw salt and bran into the fire tripod. The salt and bran crackled and spluttered in the fire. The sound which was like firecrackers added to the happy atmosphere. While the matchmaker threw salt and brain into the fire, she wished the couple a happy life. When the fire

233

tripod was close to the audience, people swarmed forward to the tripod. They hoped that the matchmaker would throw some lucky salt and bran on their heads. In the past, when the Fire Tripod Dance was performed in the countryside, villagers with unlit torches would line both sides of the roads and wait for the fire tripod. When the fire tripod was close to them, they lit their torches from the tripod and then hurried home. The villagers held the torches high in their hands in order to show that they had got the fire of happiness. After the Fire Tripod Dance was over, people usually held a torch parade going in all directions.

235 The God of Longevity bestows his blessings.

235

236

Taboos

Quanzhou was a seaport in ancient China. In the 13th century, Marco Polo, an Italian traveller, went back to Italy by ship from this port. In his travel record, he says, "At Quanzhou Port, ships and boats came and went busily and goods were piled up mountain-high." At that time, China's pottery and porcelain, silk and tea were transported to Southeast Asia on the marine Silk Road. Spices, medicinal products and other goods from Southeast Asia were also transported to China from this road. Quanzhou had close connections with other countries at that time. Therefore, jobless people from Quanzhou went abroad to make a living. Gradually, Quanzhou became famous as the hometown of overseas Chinese.

In ancient times, ocean voyages were not very safe. Storms at sea often destroyed boats. For this reason, the cherished desire of the overseas Chinese and their relatives was to pray for safe voyages. When someone was going to go abroad, their friends and relatives would give a farewell dinner to express their wish that the traveller have a good trip. A fried whole fish must be served for dinner. Only the upper part of the fish was eaten, and no one was allowed to turn the fish over and eat the other part. If someone did this, it meant the ship would capsize.

There is a five-storey pagoda on Baogai Hill in Quanzhou Bay. On the pagoda, there is a relief sculpture of two women and a man. There is a sad legend about the three relief statues. Eight hundred years ago, a young farmer named Haisheng lived at the foot of Baogai Hill. One year, he had a poor harvest because of a serious drought. He had to go abroad to work. Before leaving, he told his wife and his young sister that he would come back in three years. Three years passed, but they had not heard from him since he had left. From then on, his wife and sister climbed to the top of the hill to watch the boats on the sea, longing to see him back. They moved many rocks up to the hill-top. Day after day, they built a pagoda with these rocks so that they could look farther from the vantage point. One day, the two women tore pieces from their clothes and wrote a letter with blood on the cloth. They hung the cloth on a kite. The kite flew to an island where Haisheng was working. After Haisheng saw the letter written in blood, he came back by boat. When the boat approached Baogai Hill, the two women recognized Haisheng. They were overjoyed. Just at that moment, a big wave hit the ship and the boat capsized. The two women wept bitterly and jumped into the sea from the hill. Later, three statues were carved in order to commemorate them. The pagoda was named the Sisters-in-Law Pagoda.

From then on, when someone residing abroad came back they would stand on the bow of the ship looking at the pagoda. The pagoda standing high on the hill is a symbol for the hopes of families to be reunited.

Another unique custom is that when someone comes back from far away, the parents,

237 There is a strong tradition of reverence for ancestors among the people of Fujian, especially those who live overseas. On a visit to their hometown, they always hold a ceremony for their ancestors.

237

wife and children will not meet them first. Usually an aunt will go out to meet the person. She lets him rest a while and makes a bowl of poached eggs with sugar. Then he goes to meet his immediate family.

Actually, the custom has a good reason behind it. Generally speaking, people who come back from far away are too excited to meet their immediate family after a long separation. They should rest a while because of the exhaustion of the journey. As well, some people may have some health problems such as high blood pressure and heart disease, so it is good for them to have a rest first. Another thing is that after a long separation, some changes may have occurred in the family. So first of all, the relatives tell what has happened during the years the person was absent. By doing so, the returning person won't be surprised at any unexpected news. This way of handling things helps to avoid sudden shocks.

Unique Customs in Hui'an

Hui'an County is only 30 kilometres away from Quanzhou. The dress of the women in the fishing villages on Chongwu Island of Hui'an County is very interesting. They wear different-coloured jackets which are very short and narrow. Their jackets are so short that they don't even cover their waistlines. They use several colourful silk belts as waistbands to tie their baggy trousers. Women wear large colourful kerchiefs on their heads. They also like to wear big bamboo hats to cover their heads. The big hats and large kerchiefs on their heads shield their faces.

There are different sayings about the costumes of the women in Hui'an. It is said that they might be descended from the Yue tribe of ancient times. Hui'an people have lived there for generations. They seldom have contacts with people outside. Today the women there still dress like this because they want to preserve their traditions.

The marriage customs are unusual. At a wedding ceremony, the bride with a red cloth covering her head and face is led by a bridesmaid to the groom's home. To the sound of firecrackers, the bride and bridesmaid walk around the bonfire in front of the bridegroom's house to drive monsters and ghosts away and to pray for safety for the family. When the bride enters the house after the wedding ceremony, the groom takes the red cloth off with a steel beam. Then the bride goes to the bridal chamber.

But the newly-married couple are not allowed to stay in the bridal chamber together. The bride usually stays with a neighbour or asks her bridesmaids to stay with her in the bridal chamber or she sits at the table alone until dawn. The groom has to stay at a friend's home for the night.

The next day, the bride calls to pay respects to her husband's ancestors and her parents-in-law. At the same time, she gives gifts to the elder members of the family and the relatives. On the morning of the third day, the bridegroom's sister leads the way to a well for the bride. The bride carries two buckets of water back.

Within five days, the bride has to obey all sorts of customs. After the five days, she can go to her mother's home. After that, the bride will live with her parents. She is only allowed to go to her husband's home on the Spring Festival, the Clear and Bright Festival and the Mid-Autumn Festival. She will continue to do this until she gives birth to the first child.

Some minority nationalities also retain the custom that women after marriage still stay at their parents' home. This may be a remnant custom from the matriarchal society. There may be some other reasons for the people in Hui'an still retaining this custom. Some said that it is because women are reluctant to leave their parents or because they are afraid of having babies. They know clearly that if they have children, they can't live a free and unrestrained life as they have done with their parents, brothers and sisters at home. Besides, they can't help their parents to support their families.

In the past, there were customs to keep the newly-married couples apart. When newly-married couples met, they were not allowed to talk. The woman looked at her husband as if he was a stranger. She lived with her parents. She could receive guests at home, but when her husband came to her parents' home, she avoided meeting him. Young village women swore to each other that they would have children several years later. A woman would be mocked if she broke her pledge.

In recent years, people in this area have had more contact with the outside world and they have been influenced by the marriage law. For these reasons, young people today refuse to obey old customs. They arrange their marriage by themselves. Old marriage customs are fast on their way out.

238   A woman of Hui'an in traditional garments. Their heads are elaborately wrapped, but their abdomens are often laid bare. Hence the label, "feudalistic head, democratic abdomen."

239   Hui'an women wear headgear in the shape of a butterfly. As butterfly is the totem of the ancient Baiyue tribe, some experts infer that the people of Hui'an are descendants of the Baiyue tribe.

239

240 Two Hui'an women are lugging stone. In the past, the men of Hui'an often stayed away from home, fishing or working in quarries. The women had to take up all the productive labour at home. For this reason, the women of Hui'an have been known for their ability to bear hardships and stand hard work.

241 Apart from productive labour, they also have to do all the household chores. They head for the well first thing in the morning to carry back enough water for the day.

241

242   The bride not only wears a headcover but also holds an umbrella over her head. Thus concealed, she walks to her bridegroom's home, accompanied by her friends.

243   After the wedding, the Hui'an woman usually does not settle down in her husband's home until she gives birth to her first child, so the well-decorated bridal room is left empty.

243

The Goddess Mazu—Guard of the Sea

The colourful fishing boats in Hui'an are usually decorated with two round large eyes on the head of the boat. The boat looks like a yellow dragon on the sea at a distance. This is a traditional decoration handed down through generations. In ancient times, people believed that the Dragon King controlled the sea. Fish, shrimps, turtles and crabs all obeyed his orders. When people went fishing, they were afraid of sharks because when a shark appeared, fish would swim away and their fishing boats would be destroyed by the shark. So they believed that their dragon boats could scare sharks away.

Another custom in the fishing villages is that red paper is pasted on boats on which auspicious words are written. Before the Spring Festival, people like to post spring couplets on gates, granaries, kitchens and also on their boats. When a new boat starts the first journey or a repaired boat starts out again or when the fishermen come back from the sea, firecrackers are set off and incense is burned to express thanks to the goddess Mazu.

According to custom, when a man comes back safely, his wife will carry a pig head, a yellow croaker, cakes, duck eggs and oranges to offer sacrifices to Mazu in a temple.

Mazu is the sea goddess. She is the idol of fishermen along China's coast. The legend about Mazu goes that in 960, a baby girl was born on Meizhou Island in Putian County. The baby did not utter a cry when she was born and in the month following her birth she was named the Silent Girl. She was kind and bright. She learned how to swim from a Buddhist monk and she could walk on the water and would not sink. At the age of 15, when she heard that boats were always destroyed by submerged rocks or sank because of whirlpools, she went out to sea on a small boat. She guided the way for fishermen and helped them when they had difficulties.

At the age of 28, when she heard that a fishing boat had capsized because of a sudden storm, she went out to the sea to save the fishermen. She saved many fishermen, but then she died of exhaustion. A temple and a statue were built in order to commemorate her.

After that, there were many stories about the goddess Mazu. An ancient book *Records on the Sea* says that when fishermen were in danger, Mazu would try her best to help them. She would send heavenly soldiers to help them or went herself to save them.

244   A fishing village. The houses are built of granite in order to withstand typhoons.

244

245

246

245   The dress of fisherwomen is characterized by a close-fitting waist, narrow cuffs and wide trouser legs. The upper garment is made tight so that it cannot be lifted by the wind, and the loose trouser legs are often rolled up when wading through water.

246   The fisherwomen in Quanzhou like to wear fresh flowers in their hair. In the coastal area around Xiamen, silver headwear is preferred.

247   Mending nets is the daily work for fisherwomen.

This story is from the imagination of ancient people, but it spread far and wide among the fishermen.

Fishermen from China's mainland said that when they met fishermen from Taiwan at sea, they often saw a picture of the goddess Mazu in the drivers' cab on the boat. Taiwanese fishermen burn incense before they go out to sea and pray to Mazu to protect them.

Three hundred years ago, when some villagers in Putian moved to Taiwan, they built a statue of Mazu and took it with them to Taiwan. From then on, the goddess Mazu has become the idol of the fishermen in Tawian as well as in Fujian. Today many places in Taiwan have temples dedicated to Mazu. They always burn incense before her statue to express their respect for the goddess, and also express their thoughts of their native land.

248

249

248   Before setting sail, a fishing boat has to take enough fresh water for the day.

249   Worshipping the head of the Sea God. From the fourteenth to the sixteenth of the first lunar month, fishermen in Lianjiang County hold the ceremony of "bidding farewell to the Sea God." According to a local legend, a prince of the Dragon King who sympathized with the hardships of fishermen often informed them beforehand when his father was going to create wind and waves. Enraged, the Dragon King had the prince cleft into three pieces; one piece was preserved in the sea and the other two were thrown to Lianjiang and Mazu. In gratitude to the prince, the fishermen have worshipped him as a Sea God ever since. When the occasion comes, every household makes a head of the Sea God with paper and pays respects to it. After that, they burn it by the coast and throw the ashes into the sea, signifying the return of the Sea God to the palace of the Dragon King.

250   The entire village assembles at the bank for the ceremony of immolating the heads of the Sea God.

250

251 Riding on small boats, the
villagers scatter the ashes into the
sea and pray for the Sea God's
blessing for bumper catches and
the safety of the ships and
fishermen at sea.

251

252　Tales about the Goddess Mazu are popular among the people in the form of drama, painting and literary works. The following are four pictures from a scroll painting, *The Sacred Traces of Mazu*, done by an anonymous Qing Dynasty artist and kept in the Dajifengtang Temple in Xianyou County:

1) One day when she was sixteen, Mazu and some of her friends went to a well and examined their make-up from their own reflections in the water. A deity with a copper charm in one hand suddenly emerged from under the water. While her friends ran away in a panic, Mazu remained where she was. The deity gave her the charm, which imbued her with supernatural power since then.

2) One day when Mazu's father and brother were out on a fishing trip, a storm rose, threatening to capsize their boat. Mazu, who was weaving at home, used her charm in their rescue. Consequently her father was saved from the jaws of death, although her brother was drowned.

3) When a merchant ship ran up on a rock near Meizhou Island, Mazu threw several blades of grass into the sea, preventing the boat from sinking.

4) There were two demons in the northwest of Meizhou, one capable of hearing voices of a long distance off and the other capable of seeing things miles away. As the two often created troubles for the local people, Mazu, at the latter's request, subdued them and made them her subordinate generals.

見玄通

自是法力日

大后受之不疑

奔

符旛井而上諸女駭

井忽見神人捧銅

大后少時從群女窺

龍泉井

神救父兄
大后神救上出

将
之为
天后收伏
治于
作祟村民苦甚求
西北方有金水二精

253 A, B   The Temple of the
Goddess Mazu was built on
Meizhou Island of Fujian Province
in 987, the year in which Lin
Moniang "ascended to heaven."
The statue of the Goddess Mazu in
the temple.

253A

253B

254

255

254   The Temple of the Goddess Mazu on Meizhou Island is the first of its kind. It has given statues of the goddess to numerous other temples in China's coastal regions and in Southeast Asia.

255   Older women of Meizhou Island make a knot in their hair in the shape of a sail, reputedly modelled after the hairstyle of the Goddess Mazu.

256   Inhabitants of the coastal regions believe that Mazu is not only a goddess guarding the sea but can also regulate wind and rain, endow women with children and dispel evil spirits. Therefore many people come to burn incense at the temple.

256

257   The twenty-third of the third lunar month is the birthday of Mazu. On this day, grand sacrificial ceremonies are held in Fujian, Taiwan, Hong Kong, the Bohai coast and some areas in Southeast Asia. There are also parades with dragon-dances, people walking on stilts, folk music accompanied by drumbeats and variety shows. This pictures shows the dragon-dance performance in a fishing village in Fujian to commemorate the birthday of Mazu.

257

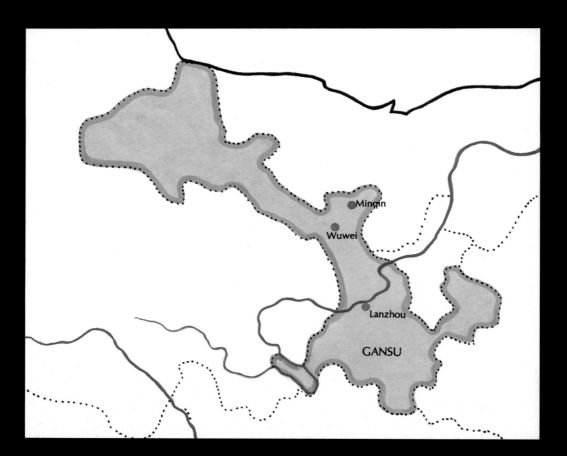

X. Customs on the Silk Road

G ANSU Province in Northwest China, intersected by the Silk Road that linked Europe and Asia in ancient times, is a vital communication line connecting the interior with the northwestern border areas of China. Many interesting and unique customs can be seen in Gansu Province, some of which have been handed down from the time when the Silk Road was bustling with travellers.

Sheepskin Rafts on the Yellow River

After having passed the provincial capital of the city of Lanzhou, the Yellow River runs through Gansu Province. The sheepskin raft, an ancient ferry, has a unique structure and is easily made. First make a sheepskin bag, which should be made with the whole skin from a sheep. The wool should be shaved from the skin. After the skin is dried, salt and sesame oil are spread on it and it is rubbed with both hands. Then it is scrubbed with tung oil. The skin is tied lightly into a bag with ropes, except the opening on the front leg, through which air will be blown in. Bind the blown-up sheepskin bags onto a wooden frame. Then the raft is ready.

Sheepskin rafts come in various sizes, some made of over a dozen sheepskin bags, some a few dozen bags, and others several hundred bags. A small raft can hold a few people and a big raft can transport several tons of goods and can sail at a daily speed of 200 kilometres with the current. In the swiftly-running Yellow River, the raft can only move along with the current, but it can't go against the current. Therefore the boatman often walks for a while towards the upper reaches, carrying a sheepskin raft, before he puts it into the river and lets it float to the other side of the river.

Today though there are motor-driven boats on the Yellow River and bridges at important sites, the sheepskin rafts can still be seen on the river. Taking a raft is convenient, because the raft only weighs a bit more than 12 kilogrammes and can be carried on the shoulder to cross the river instead of taking a detour across a bridge. In addition, each household raises sheep. It does not require much money to construct a raft.

Though it can be tossed about by the waves of the Yellow River, the raft is safe. The Yellow River is full of swift currents and dangerous shoals. Because it has some elasticity, the raft will be bumped back when it runs into a reef. If one or two sheepskin bags on the raft break, the raft will not sink.

258 An old-style water wheel on the Yellow River. Propelled by the currents, it lifts water to irrigate the cultivated fields.

259 A, B Villagers who live by the Yellow River make rafts with sheepskin. They inflate sheepskins and then bind them to a wooden frame.

259 A

259 B

234

260   Sheepskin rafts are lined up at a ford of the Yellow River. Each raft can carry five or six people.

261   Tied behind the raft, mules and horses can be transported across the river.

261

Mid-Autumn Festival in Ancient Liangzhou

Wuwei, called Liangzhou in ancient times, is 200 kilometres north from Lanzhou and was once an important town on the Silk Road. When we arrived at Wuwei, it was the

262 Villagers in Gansu make mooncakes at home for the Mid-Autumn Festival. Each household makes its own mooncakes with their own particular pattern, filling and flavour.

262

Mid-Autumn Festival, which falls on the 15th day of the eighth lunar month. Looking at the moon in the courtyard of a farmer's house was lovely because the moon at the Mid-Autumn Festival is the brightest in the year. According to Chinese custom, every family places a table on which to burn incense in the courtyard on that day, which holds mooncakes, melons and fruits. The whole family often sit around the table eating mooncakes, while appreciating the full moon. The festival is a time for family reunions.

Appreciating the full moon can be traced back to the Zhou Dynasty 3,000 years ago, when the Son of Heaven offered sacrifices to the sun to welcome spring on the 15th day of the second lunar month and to the moon to welcome winter on the 15th day of the eighth lunar month, praying for favourable weather and good harvests. It was not until the Tang Dynasty (618–907) when the Mid-Autumn Festival was officially designated, that the festival became popular among the people. Mooncakes are special for the Mid-Autumn Festival. China boasts more than 150 varieties of mooncakes made in various ways with different ingredients. Each variety of mooncakes produced by different places has its own distinct flavour. The mooncakes of Jiangsu are crisp with many layers; those of Beijing are mainly made of vegetable oil and stuffed with vegetable fillings; and those of Guangzhou are known for their tasty fillings made of shredded coconut, lotus seeds, yolk and ham. Mooncakes made by local peasants in Liangzhou are especially big, looking like big millstones when peasants carry them on their bikes. The largest one is one metre in diameter. Some of the Liangzhou mooncakes are laced with flour petals in addition to a white flour rabbit in the centre of the cake. There is a fairy tale about the rabbit.

Legend has it that Chang'e lived in the Moon Palace. She was the wife of Hou Yi. Hou Yi was a legendary hero, who saved people from drought by shooting down nine suns from the sky. However, he became a tyrant after he became king. One day his wife, Chang'e, learnt that he had obtained a herb which made a person immortal. She knew that anyone who took the herb would live forever. Afraid her husband would rule the people cruelly forever, she stole his herb and took it herself. To her surprise, she soon became light and flew to the Moon Palace. The rabbit was Chang'e's pet, and went to the moon together with Chang'e.

On the evening of the festival, each family in Liangzhou spreads homemade mooncakes, apples, grapes, pears, water melons and other foods on a table. The table is moved to the courtyard. Housewives visit with each other to taste mooncakes and judge whose are the best.

When the full moon comes out, housewives burn incense and light candles to offer sacrifices to the goddess in the moon, Chang'e. Among local people however, the men traditionally do not pay homage to the moon.

After the ceremony, the eldest member of the family will cut the cake into pieces and divide them among family members. However, according to the local Liangzhou custom, people don't eat the cake until the next evening. This custom has its roots in the history of Liangzhou. In ancient times, Liangzhou was the place where disgraced officials and criminals were exiled. Those who were far away from their homes missed their family very much. At the Mid-Autumn Festival, looking at the bright moon, more than ever they thought of their families far away. So they didn't eat all the mooncakes at once for they were a symbol of the family reunion.

237

263

263 Gifts of mooncakes are exchanged at the Mid-Autumn Festival to symbolize family harmony for all the four seasons. This mooncake given as a gift is the size of a basin.

264 Offering a sacrifice to the moon on the night of the Mid-Autumn Festival.

264

265 Minqin County is surrounded by desert on three sides. The courtyards in the villages are all girdled by high walls to resist wind and sand. They are therefore called "village castles." The picture shows a castle–like house whose wall is comparable with ancient city walls.

265

Local Fast Food—Steamed Bread in Watermelon Juice

Minqin County is surrounded by desert on three sides. Two thirds of the county is covered by sand. At oases in the desert large sweet watermelons and Lanzhou honey melons grow thanks to the long hours of sunshine and the great disparity in temperature between day and night.

To eat a melon it is necessary only to press the melon with the thumb, and the melon will split in the middle.

Then the melon is stirred with chopsticks into juice, and griddle cakes or steamed bread are broken into pieces with the hands and soaked in the melon juice. Soon afterwards, the bread will become soft and will be ready to eat. Sweet, cool and refreshing, steamed bread in watermelon juice is a common food in Liangzhou.

In summer and autumn, whether herding livestock on the grasslands, threshing the crops, shopping in a town, or watching open–air performances, people often carry some steamed bread and watermelons with a *dalian* (a long rectangular bag sewn up at both ends with an opening in the middle) on their shoulders. When they feel hungry, it is very convenient for them to eat this fast food.

Students who study far away often carry two bags. One is a schoolbag and the other is for watermelons and food. More often than not two naughty boys open a melon along the way, eating while walking. Halfway to school they have already eaten up half of their lunch.

266   The houses inside the castle are well-ordered and secure.

267   Village women in Gansu wrap their heads, foreheads and ears with a square towel to protect themselves from the sandstorms.

266

267

268   Wuwei is famous for peppers. In autumn, the courtyard and rooftops of every village household are strewn with red peppers.

268

269

270

271

272

269   Persimmons there are fleshy and sweet. On reaching maturity in autumn, they are strung together to be aired and finally flattened into dried persimmon.

270   The family are having a regular meal—steamed bread soaked in watermelon juice.

271   Watermelon stalls such as this can be found on any highway running across yellow sand away from village or town. To relish "steamed bread in watermelon juice" on their way, travellers along the Silk Road only have to bring steamed bread with them.

272   Donkey and ox carts remain the major vehicles of transportation in rural Gansu.

273   This is the rubbing of a stone carving excavated from an ancient tomb at the Jiayu Pass at the west end of the Great Wall. The ox cart looks exactly the same as those used today.

274   Relics of the Great Wall run across Gansu Province. The picture shows a shepherd herding sheep under a stretch of the wall.

243

273

Clowns Teasing the Bride

Fortunately we had a chance to attend a local wedding ceremony in Yongfeng Village in Minqin County. Soon after noon, two small transport tractors decorated with red silk scarves made their way slowly to the front of the bride's home. The bride and bridegroom sat on one tractor and the dowry was put on the other tractor. Following the two tractors were several dozen bikes ridden by relatives and friends of the couple. However, it was strange that the procession was stopped at the gate of the bride's home by two clowns wearing paper hats, shabby leather jackets and covered with colourful bedsheets, with red peppers hung on their ears.

At the wedding ceremony, the elders should be dignified and the youngers should be courteous. How to make the wedding fun was the question. Inspired by the clowns of traditional operas, the groom's older brothers dress up as opera clowns, performing tricks and antics to liven up the atmosphere of the wedding. First, the clowns ask the bride for a gift and the bride will give them each a traditional embroidered box. But when the bride is about to enter the front gate of the house, she will be stopped again. Some people put saddles in front of the couple. When the newlyweds sit on the saddles, the master of the ceremony will sing: "After the new couple stride the saddles together, they will be safe for life." In this way people wish the new couple happiness, safety and good health because saddle and safe sound the same in Chinese.

As soon as the bride enters the gate of her husband's home, his sister-in-law will hand her new clothes and embroidered shoes. According to the local custom, so long as the bride puts on new clothes and the shoes from her husband's home, she can be a member of her husband's family and is allowed to enter the bridal chamber.

In North China, after the bride has taken her seat in the bridal chamber, her mother-in-law will spread dates and chestnuts on her, wishing her to have children soon. Sometimes, the father-in-law scatters cigarettes on the bed, symbolizing a growing

275   A decorated carriage takes the bride to the house of the bridegroom.

275

276   At the wedding, the elder brother of the bridegroom plays the clown to entertain the guests and relieve the bashful bride.

277   On the second day of her marriage, the bride had to demonstrate her culinary skills by preparing meat soup for her parents-in-law and other members of her husband's family. This ancient tradition still persists in Gansu, though the meat soup has been replaced by noodles.

277

family. However, Minqin County does not produce dates and chestnuts, so people use turnips and steamed bread to symbolize plump children. The morning following the wedding, the two younger brothers of the groom knock at the door and when the bride opens the door, two turnips will be thrown into her arms. Not long afterwards, the mother-in-law also comes to give her steamed bread which symbolizes her hope for a grandchild.

The day after the wedding, the bride will do some cooking to show her ability to do housework. After she has prepared noodles, she will present them respectfully to her parents-in-law. In return, her mother-in-law gives her clothes and money. When the bride serves her new brothers-in-law dressed up as clowns, they will continue teasing her, so as to make the bride feel at ease.

It is customary that the newlyweds go to the well to fetch water the day after the wedding. When they come back to the house, two clowns will jump out at them and throw stones into their buckets, splashing water on the new couple. This trick is called sinking stones, which is a homonym for the word honest in Chinese, symbolizing the wish that their sister-in-law be an honest woman.

278 A memorial hall for the dead, where family members and relatives come to offer condolences and pay their last respects.

279 The night before the burial, people set out towards the uncultivated land, carrying torches, to locate and dig the pit.

280 Two paper cranes are placed above the coffin in the hope that the dead person will ride the cranes to heaven.

281 The funeral procession heads for the burial ground to the accompaniment of the doleful music of *suona* horns.

279

280

281

282 A caravan of camels trekking
in the desert.

282

Camel Trains in the Desert

The camel is known as the "boat of the desert." In the past two thousand years, caravans on the Silk Road transported silk, tea, pottery and lacquerware from China to the western regions and pearls, jade, herbal medicines and perfume from Central and West Asia and Europe to China.

Peasants in Minqin County raise camels in their spare time. In summer they milk camels and collect camel hair and in autumn, they earn money by using camels to transport goods.

Camels do not like hot weather. Usually camel trains do not set off until the cool autumn comes around. In the 1950s, a railroad was built in the Hexi Corridor, and highways radiated in all directions. Since then, camel trains for long–distance transportation have disappeared. Caravans are now used only to transport grain, tea, cloth and other goods to the herdsmen in the deserts.

Usually the camel train sets off in the afternoon. Before its departure, the grooms load goods on the camels with the head camel carrying tents, grain, kitchen utensils and water. When everything is ready, the grooms link the camels by tying the rope tied on the camel's nose onto the saddle of the lead camel. Four grooms will travel in a group, leading a cavaran of 28 camels.

First of all the camel train will walk in between two bonfires. In the past, when travelling in the desert, grooms often met natural and man–made calamities, such as storms, dry weather, wild animals, illnesses and bandits. Powerless, the grooms could do nothing but pray for good fortune. They believed that if they walked in between two bonfires, all disasters and illnesses could be driven off.

The bells accompanying the camel caravans in the desert have provided interesting themes for poems, paintings and music. Instead of being hung on the camel's neck, bells in the shape of an iron bucket are hung on a stick on the saddle of the last camel. In the vast and silent deserts, the sound of slow and rhythmic camel bells is the only music for the grooms. However, the real purpose of using the bells is to prevent camels from being lost. Camels are very timid. Even when a hare passes by, it will be frightened and jump. To avoid breaking the camel's nose, a knot which can be undone by a pull is tied

283

284 After a long journey, they come upon a clear stream.

284

on each camel's nose. So a startled camel may leave the caravan without the groom's knowledge. But if grooms who walk ahead of the camel train don't hear the bells, they will know that the camels are lost and will look for them.

In addition, the bells can be used as the signal of the camel train. In the past, bandits often robbed goods on the way. When approaching dangerous spots, grooms would hide the bells. Without hearing the familiar sound, camels would know that their masters wanted them to keep on without making noise.

The bells can also be used as alarm bells. Upon hearing the bells, foxes, hares and gerbils that come out to look for food will escape in a hurry or hide in holes. Thus they will not disturb the camels.

Camels are loyal companions and guides to desert travellers. Before a storm, alert camels will lie on the ground. The grooms stay close to them to avoid the onslaught of the storm. In addition, camels often guide grooms to water sources. Therefore those who raise camels look after them well as they depend on them for survival at times. For example, as camels do not like hot weather, grooms often start their journey at nightfall and stop travelling at midnight in order to avoid the scorching sun of the day. For fear that the hard stones of the roads will hurt the hooves of the camel, they often carefully choose good roads, and even take the trouble of walking through deserts. If they have to take asphalt roads or natural paths, they will protect the hooves of the camels by tying soft sheepskin onto them.

253

285

285   A caravan of camels on journey.

XI. Attractions of Lingnan

IN South China lies a mountain chain on the border of Guangxi and Guangdong provinces and the border of Hunan and Jiangxi provinces. The mountains are called the Nanling Mountains, and extend from northeast to southwest, with an average elevation of over 1,000 metres. The area to the south of the Nanling Mountains is called Lingnan (South of the Range). With the Nanling Mountains to the north and facing the South China Sea in the south, Guangdong is an interesting province with customs quite different from those of the interior.

Flower Fair at Spring Festival Time

Guangzhou, the capital of Guangdong Province, is a beautiful old city. Legend has it that in ancient times five immortals in colourful clothes once descended on to Guangzhou on five rams. On their departure, each of them left a rice ear, expressing the wish that Guangzhou would be forever free from famine. Hence Guangzhou is also known as the City of Rams and the City of Rice Ears. A stone sculpture of five rams on Yuexiu Hill in the centre of the city had become the emblem of the city.

Walking along the streets of Guangzhou, I was immediately taken by the vegetable stalls under green and luxuriant trees selling all kinds of greens. Thinking of cold Beijing where piles of cabbages for winter were covered with thick quilts, I could not help but notice the difference.

When the Spring Festival approaches, the streets and fairs bustle with people shopping and florists from suburban areas setting up temporary shacks for the flower fair.

Guangzhou is known for its flower fair held annually during the Spring Festival. The fair in the centre of the city is one of Guangzhou's six major flower fairs. The streets are decorated with fragrant and beautiful fresh flowers, golden tangerines, and elegant miniature landscapes, looking like rivers of flowers in the distance. If we connected the flower stalls, there would be a flower street stretching for miles.

It is the Chinese tradition to welcome spring with flowers. North China is cold in spring, so flowers don't bloom outdoors. People there decorate their homes with miniature landscapes and potted flowers to add to the festival atmosphere. Country girls like to cut red paper into peach and plum blossoms and paste them onto doors and windows and they use red velvet flowers as ornaments on their upswept hair or at the ends of braids. With a warm and wet climate, Guangzhou has fresh flowers all year round. The origin of flower fairs can be traced back 500 years. From then on, flower fairs were held in Guangzhou during the Spring Festival every year. There is an old saying there, "No flower fairs, no Spring Festival."

It is customary to visit the flower fair on the eve of the Spring Festival and buy a potted tree with tangerines hanging on it. People also put colourful flowers into vases. Immediately, the sitting room will be fragrant and pleasing to the eye. In addition, the tangerine symbolizes good luck and wealth to the local people and the chrysanthemum symbolizes longevity. On the contrary, if one comes back from the flower fair empty-handed amidst the sound of firecrackers when a year ends, one will feel unhappy. All unhappiness in the following year will be attributed to not having bought flowers at the fair.

256

286

286, 287   Fresh flowers adorn streets, lanes, courtyards and balconies in Guangzhou.

287

288

288 In the outskirts of Guangzhou there are many households or even whole villages solely engaged in the cultivation of flowers for the market. These flowers not only supply the market in Guangzhou but are also sold to other cities and provinces. The picture shows a residential quarter of the florists in Chen Village, Shunde County.

289, 290 Along the street, flowers are arranged into a variety of pictures and beloved figures from popular legends.

289

290

291

291   During the Spring Festival, the flower market is open round the clock.

292   On their daily shopping sallies, housewives often buy a bunch of fresh flowers to decorate their houses.

292

293 A special tea set, usually made of purple pottery, is used for drinking *gongfu* tea. A large pot is used for boiling water, and a smaller one for pouring tea. Teacups are very small. There is a set formula for the entire procedure from boiling water to filling the cups and drinking the tea, which can be called the Chinese tea ceremony.

294 Water must be boiled over charcoal fire from a porcelain stove.

295 Pour boiling water into the small teapot.

293

294

295

296 Pour tea into the cup.

296

Drinking *Gongfu* Tea

It is a Chinese custom to treat guests with tea. However, people in east Guangdong and south Fujian have a special way of preparing tea, called *gongfu* tea.

The tea sets from making *gongfu* tea are very small. The pottery teapot is as big as a fist and the white and transparent teacups are as small as tiny liqueur glasses. In addition they use a small charcoal stove, a small water kettle and a porcelain base for holding tea sets. Spring or well water is the best for making *gongfu* tea. Water is boiled with olive stones, which give out high flames and the delicate fragrance of olives. Before making tea, first the teapot is cleaned with boiled water to get rid of the remaining tea flavour in the pot and make better tea with a warm teapot. Then a big handful of tea leaves is put into the teapot till they almost reach its rim.

After the water is boiled, one must lift the kettle high to pour hot water into the teapot. The water is continually poured even when it overflows, so as to get rid of impure materials and foam, and to make mellow tea. After the lid is put on the teapot, boiling water is poured onto the teapot. In this way, the tea will swell in no time. A few minutes later, the tea can be poured into the cups which are arranged in a circle. The way to pour tea is special. It is poured with a circular motion into each cup. In this way, the colour and consistency of the tea in all the cups are the same. To avoid creating foam and scattering the fragrance of tea, the teapot should be held close to the teacups. When the tea is ready, the teacups are presented to guests and elders with both hands.

It is mentally refreshing to see the yellow and limpid tea and smell its delicate fragrance. The first sip seems slightly bitter, but a while later, the sweetness of the tea can be savoured.

297   When the host is pouring tea, the guest expresses his thanks by knocking on the table with his index and middle fingers.

298   Several old people drink *gongfu* tea in the courtyard.

299   *Gongfu* tea is also popular in Fujian Province to the east of Guangdong Province. Different styles of tea sets are used in different areas. The picture shows the conventional tea set in eastern Fujian. Each teacup has a cover and a wooden tray.

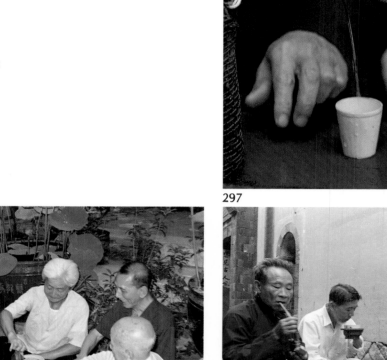

297

298

299

Wulong (black dragon) tea is the best variety for making *gongfu* tea. Half fermented, Wulong tea is as mellow as black tea and as refreshing and sweet as green tea, complete with lingering aftertaste. According to research, Wulong tea helps prevent and cure illnesses, prolong life and prevent arteriosclerosis and cancer.

Guangdong's Wulong tea comes from Anxi in Fujian Province. Legend has it that the first cultivator of the tea was named Wu Liang. One day, Wu Liang went to the mountains, carrying a tea basket on his back and a hunting gun. He went home after he had picked several pounds of mountain tea and caught a river deer. In the evening, he was busy with killing the river deer, and didn't have enough time to dry the green tea. The next day, he found the tea in the basket had fermented on the way back and after having been stored in the basket the whole night. He fried the tea at once. To his surprise, he found that the tea tasted very mellow, with no bitter and astringent taste. Soon Wu Liang taught his fellow villagers how to make the tea. Almost everyone in his village liked the fermented tea and they named it Wu Liang tea. In the south Fujian dialect, *liang* and *long* are two homophonic words. As time went by the tea was called Wulong tea by later generations.

Customs of the Hakkas

With a population of about 40 million, the Hakkas are spread throughout many provinces in South China, such as Guangdong, Fujian, Jiangxi, Hunan, Guangxi, Sichuan, Taiwan and Hainan. The Hakkas used to be the northern Hans living in Shanxi, Henan and Hebei. During the 200 to 300 years after the third century, there were constant wars in North China resulting in frequent changes of rulers. The northern Hans who were plagued by wars and disasters could not stay there anymore and had to abandon their homes. They crossed the Yellow and Yangtze rivers in groups, moving towards the south little by little. Finally they settled down in South China. It is called the first immigration in Chinese history. At the end of the Tang Dynasty in the ninth century and at the end of the Southern Song in the thirteenth century, China experienced another two immigrations because of wars. With knowledge of the origin and path of these three immigrations, an immigration history of the Chinese nation can be outlined.

The Hakkas who immigrated to the south cherish their own traditions. They retain their own language, culture, rites and customs. Isolated by the high mountains, they did not have much contact with local inhabitants. As a result, they have their own unique customs.

The Hakkas make a beancurd dish on festivals and for the lunar New Year, filling each small piece of beancurd with ground meat and then frying them until they become brown, and finally they are put into a pot for cooking. They did this because when the northerners moved to South China, they were short of flour to make *jiaozi* (dumplings with meat and vegetable stuffing) at festival times, so they made stuffed beancurd instead to adapt to the new conditions.

The Hakka dialect is one of seven major dialects in China. Compared with the other two main local dialects (Guangzhou and southern Fujian dialects), Hakka is the most similar to Putonghua (standard Mandarin Chinese).

Folk songs are popular among the Hakkas. When cutting firewood in the mountains, or taking a break during work, young people will sing in antiphonal style with high voices. Their songs are about the land, work and life. Love songs are also popular. The following song is an example:

> Seeing vines twine around trees when one enters the mountains,
> And finding trees and vines tangled together when one leaves.
> If trees are dead, vines will stay with them forever,
> And If vines die, trees will refuse to abandon them unless they did too.

Here trees and vines are likened to affectionate couples, ready to sacrifice for each other. The origin of the folk songs can be found in the *Book of Songs* edited by Confucius. The folk songs in the book were collected from Shanxi, Hebei and Henan provinces.

The funeral rites for the Hakkas are unique. When someone dies, southerners place the body in a coffin and bury the coffin with a tombstone in front of the tomb. Then the funeral is finished. However, the Hakkas dig up the coffin three to five years later to clean the remains of the dead. The Hakkas call the rite "leading ancestors from underground." Then they place the remains of the body into the shape of a man, bend his limbs and store them in a pottery jar and bury the jar in a selected spot. It is called the second burial by archaeologists. It is said that this rite should be attributed to the immigration of the Hakkas to the south. No matter where they went, the men in the family would carry the ancestors' remains. As soon as they had settled down in a place, they would bury their ancestors, because they were afraid that they would not be able to go back to their hometown to pay respects to their dead ancestors if they moved far away from home.

The Hakkas, who were forced to leave home and wandered about, adopt various ways to express their desire of living and working in peace and contentment. When a couple is married, people will find a bunch of grass tied with a red string in a basket and hung at the head of the bed in the bridal chamber. The grass, called "longevity grass," is brought by the bride and must be planted in the vegetable garden of her husband's family on the wedding day, symbolizing that she will take root there and will not move in her later life.

The houses of the Hakkas show that they abide by their old tradition and refuse to be assimilated. A house usually holds several dozen to a hundred families. One can imagine that the architect must take pains to design such a huge project which embraces so many people.

In square, rectangular, semicircular and round shapes, the surrounding houses or buildings often have two or three storeys with windows facing outside and the door facing inside. Some houses have two to three circles of surrounding structures. The rooms upstairs and downstairs serve as bedrooms, kitchens, storage places and livestock sheds. Between the buildings are courtyards where residents dry things on sunny days, drain water on rainy days, or hold outdoor activities. In case of fire, the lanes around the walls and the courtyards help to prevent the fire from spreading.

The layout of each building is different. With some, the front door, portico, courtyard, middle hall and main hall are the central axis with chambers, living rooms and courtyards arranged symmetrically on both sides. Some use the middle hall as an ancestral hall, which is flanked by chambers and backs on to two or three semi–circular surrounding buildings.

There is a pond in front of each house for collecting water drained from the courtyard. People raise fish and wash clothes and vegetables in the pond and water the vegetable garden with the water from the pond. If there is a fire, the water from the pond is used to put it out.

The ancestral hall is the heart of a house. On festivals, families make sacrificial offerings to their ancestors. Anyone from the family who comes home from far away or is going to marry must go to the ancestral hall to pay respects to their forefathers. So do girls who are going to marry in another place or members of the family who are leaving home. It also serves as a mourning hall if one of the family elders dies. With their own unique structures, the surrounding buildings of the Hakkas are suitable for family life, although as in any living arrangement, disputes and conflicts among several dozen families living in a huge house are unavoidable. Therefore, a respected member of the community is elected as the leader of the group. Collective decisions are made on weddings or funerals, schools, water conservancy projects, repairs on bridges and roads and other decisions affecting the group. However, if anyone violates the clan's rules or discipline, or if the village comes into conflict with another village, the clan head will take measures to handle it.

To keep peace in the village, local people abide by unwritten rules which are understood. People living in the earth buildings may pile and store things in front of their rooms, but are not allowed to occupy the territory belonging to other people. In the season for transplanting rice sprouts, people should use the water equally, so that every family can transplant rice sprouts on time. If anyone keeps water for his own use, the clan head has the right to open breaches along the ditch. If one injures a person in the fight for water, he must pay all medical expenses for the injured and go to his home

300　Most of the Hakkas are congregated in eastern Guangdong and the mountain areas of western Fujian.

263

300

to apologize. When the rice is ripe, it is prohibited to release chickens and ducks to the fields. If anyone who acts against the rules, his chickens or ducks can be eaten by anyone who catches them. In the mountains forests are important sources of income. Those who secretly cut timbers shall pay for the wood according to arranged prices. Those who start forest fires out of carelessness shall hold banquets to treat the villagers who help put out the fire, and made a compensatory payment according to an arranged price.

When sons grow up, the family holding will be shared among them. First of all, the father and sons discuss how to divide houses and property. When a man sets up his own household, his father-in-law will come with rice, wood and buckets in the morning amidst firecrackers. The buckets hold pots, bowls, ladles, cakes, onions, garlic and celery. They bring these in order to help their daughters and sons-in-law establish their own homes and also to express their wish that they will work hard and earn their income themselves (celery, onion, garlic and wood being homonymous with the words for diligence, clever, calculation and wealth in Chinese).

But when small families are set up, a part of fields, mountains, forests and fish ponds will be left as public property of the whole family. The public fields will be ploughed and taken care of by sons and grandsons in turn. Income from public fields will be used to offer sacrifices to ancestors, help the poorer members of the clan, for education or to establish public facilities.

Although clan rules and rites have been replaced by government laws and regulations, the former clan rules still play an active role in maintaining the unity of a village.

301   A group of enclosed Hakka houses. The wall is propped by a frame of bamboo and wood chips. Cooked glutinous rice and brown sugar are added to immature soil, fine sand and limestone, which are kneaded, pounded, pressed, and finally rammed into place to make the wall.

302   Inner view of a round enclosed house. Usually, the first floor is used as the kitchen, the second floor for food storage, and the third floor and above as bedrooms.

302

303

303   Inner view of a square enclosed house.

304   Inner view of a semicircular enclosed house. Two arc-shaped structures are separated by the courtyard.

304

305 Illustration of the structure
of an enclosed house.

306 The ancestral hall, located in
the centre of the building, houses
the memorial tablets of the clan
ancestors and also serves as the
clan meeting-place.

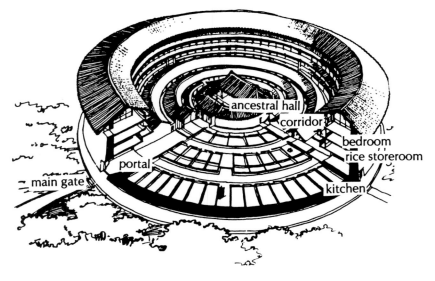

305

306

307, 308　According to Hakka custom, fir twigs and grass are placed above and on the bridal bed on the wedding day. The fir twigs are brought over by the bride's younger brother to express the wish that the new couple will soon be blessed with a son. The grass, brought by the bride herself, will be planted in the vegetable lot of her husband's family; it is called "longevity grass."

307

308

309–311 The ancient custom of a double funeral has persisted among the Hakkas. For the second funeral, the bones are put into a pottery jar, a tomb is built and a tombstone erected. The family will offer a sacrifice at the tomb every year. The pictures show scenes of the sacrificial ceremony held by the Xu clan in Jiaoling in Guangdong Province.

309

310

311

312 For the Hakkas, ancestral sacrifice is an occasion to commemorate the virtues of their ancestors and to achieve a sense of unity among the clan. Conducted on a grand scale, each family of the clan brings their share of sacrificial offerings for the ceremony.

313 Pig and lamb carcasses, incense, candles and firecrackers are all used in the ceremony.

314 Memorial tablets of the ancestors are displayed in the ancestral hall.

312

313

314

315   After sacrificial offerings are presented at the altar, people pay their respects to their ancestors by kowtowing in the sequence of seniority.

315

中 国 民 俗

丘桓兴　撰文

鲁忠民　等摄影

*

外文出版社出版

（中国北京百万庄路 24 号）

邮政编码 100037

凸版印刷（新加坡）私人有限公司印刷

中国国际图书贸易总公司发行

（中国北京车公庄西路 35 号）

北京邮政信箱第 399 号　邮政编码 100044

1992 年（小 8 开）第一版

（英）

ISBN 7—119—01471—4 / J・1111（外）

18800

85—E—388 S